Paper
Tricks
& Toys

E. Richard Churchill
Illustrated by James Michaels

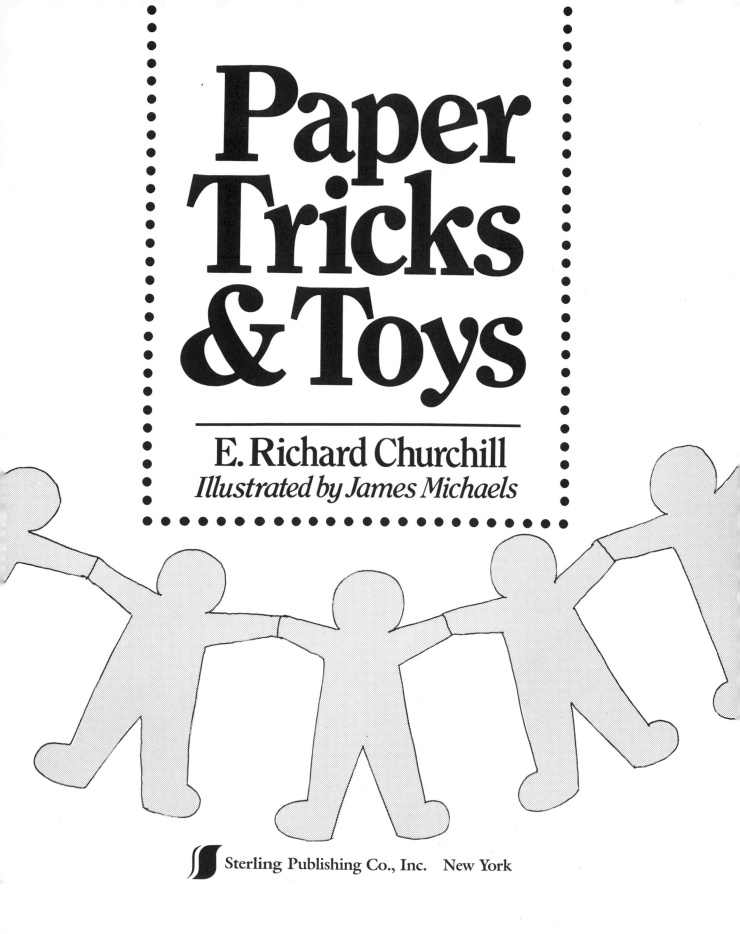

Sterling Publishing Co., Inc.   New York

For Chum, who makes every day Valentine's Day.

With special thanks to the students of Brentwood Middle School in Greeley, Colorado, who can always be counted on to supply great ideas.

Edited by Keith L. Schiffman

Library of Congress Cataloging-in-Publication Data

Churchill, E. Richard (Elmer Richard)
　　Paper tricks & toys / by E. Richard Churchill : illustrated by
James Michaels.
　　　　p.　　cm.
　　Includes index.
　　Summary: A collection of thirty-five magic tricks using folded
paper. Includes some optical illusions and some simple toys.
　　ISBN 0-8069-8416-3 (trade)
　　1. Paper work—Juvenile literature.　2. Magic—Juvenile
literature.　3. Paper toys—Juvenile literature.　[1. Paper work.
2. Magic tricks.]　I. Michaels, James, ill.　II. Title.
III. Title: Paper tricks and toys.
TT870.C5455　1992
793.8—dc20　　　　　　　　　　　　　　　　　91-38789
　　　　　　　　　　　　　　　　　　　　　　　　CIP
　　　　　　　　　　　　　　　　　　　　　　　　AC

10　9　8　7　6　5　4　3　2　1

Published in 1992 by Sterling Publishing Company, Inc.
387 Park Avenue South, New York, N.Y. 10016
© 1992 by E. Richard Churchill
Distributed in Canada by Sterling Publishing
℅ Canadian Manda Group, P.O. Box 920, Station U
Toronto, Ontario, Canada M8Z 5P9
Distributed in Great Britain and Europe by Cassell PLC
Villiers House, 41/47 Strand, London WC2N 5JE, England
Distributed in Australia by Capricorn Link Ltd.
P.O. Box 665, Lane Cove, NSW 2066
Manufactured in the United States of America
All rights reserved

Sterling ISBN 0-8069-8416-3 Trade

CONTENTS

FOLDED PAPER CAN BE TRICKY

Do you enjoy playing tricks on others? Do you get a kick out of making a few folds in a sheet of paper and turning the paper into something surprising?

Is it fun to change a piece of paper or two into a quick magic trick? Would you enjoy making a paper puzzle to entertain and amuse yourself and your friends?

Do you have a good time stumping your friends as they wonder what great stunt, trick, or toy you'll come up with next?

If you've answered "yes" to any or all of these questions, then read on. This book is for you!

TRICKY PAPER SURPRISES

Each project in this chapter turns into a paper surprise. They may trap you, puzzle you, or even astonish you and your friends.

Two will surprise you with their noise, and a couple will give you a great chance to play harmless tricks on your friends.

TRICKY FINGER TRAP

Begin with a piece of paper 11″ or 12″ long and 6″ wide. A finger trap made of notebook paper or typing paper will work just fine. Make an even better finger trap using heavy brown paper cut from the side of a grocery bag. The tougher the paper, the better the trap.

Make two scissor cuts in the paper as shown in Illus. 1. These cuts should be 6″ long. As you can see from the drawing, each cut is 2″ from the edge of the paper. This means that there will be 2″ between the cuts, as well.

Once the cuts are made, begin rolling the paper into a tube about ½″ across. Roll the cut ends first. The loose ends will end up inside the tube once you've rolled the entire sheet into a tube. Illus. 2 shows the rolling job just getting started.

Take your time making the tube. The three loose ends of paper must become part of the finger trap. It helps to have an extra hand when you first start rolling those loose paper ends. When the tube is finished, fasten the loose edge with three strips of tape. Illus. 3 shows the finished tube.

Stick the index finger of each hand into the two open ends of the tube, as shown in Illus. 4. Push your fingers into the tube all the way. If the tube isn't nice and tight around your fingers, reroll the tube and make it a little smaller.

Once you've pushed your fingers into the tube, pull them straight out, if you can. The trap should hold your fingers tight, and it should refuse to release them.

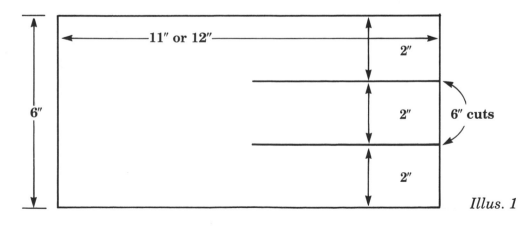

Illus. 1

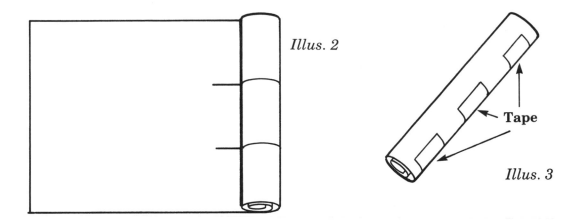

Illus. 2

Tape

Illus. 3

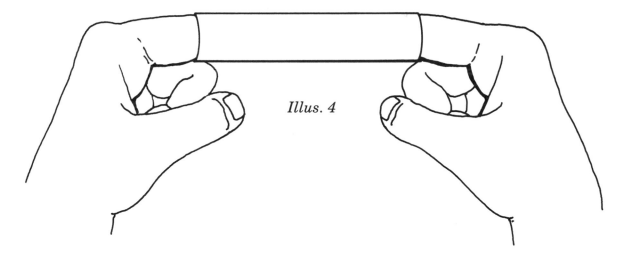

Illus. 4

Don't panic. You don't have to destroy the trap to get free. Just push your fingers back towards the middle of the tube. Now, one at a time, ease your fingers out of the trap.

The trick is to make certain you roll the tube so that it's large enough for your fingers to slip in and tight enough so that your fingers completely fill the tube once they're pushed in as far as they can go.

Try your *Tricky Finger Trap* on your friends. Don't get upset when someone rips a trap apart, trying to pull free. Make another trap, and then go looking for new fingers to capture!

Hey buddy, need an extra hand to fold that?

TWO-PIECE PAPER POPPER

Paper poppers are great fun. The noise they make adds a lot to any day! Teachers *hate* to hear them in the hallways and parents *hate* hearing poppers crack and bang for hours at a time. Here's your chance to be an obnoxious pest!

For your *Two-Piece Paper Popper* you need a 6″ square of really stiff paper. Lightweight cardboard from the side of a cereal box is even better. A square cut from an old file folder is excellent. Heavy construction paper will work just fine.

You also need a small square of lighter paper. A 4″ square of notebook paper will do the job nicely.

Begin by folding both squares diagonally so they look like the drawing shown in Illus. 5.

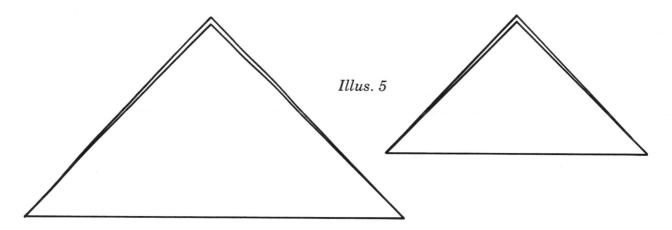

Illus. 5

Set the larger square aside for just a minute. While the smaller square is still folded, cut off one corner, as shown in Illus. 6. Cut off about ½″.

Unfold the paper, and it should look like Illus. 7. The dotted lines in the drawing show where to fold up the two sides of the paper. Crease these folds, and then unfold the paper.

Now you need the larger square of material. Lay it flat so that the fold looks like a little valley. Turn the smaller

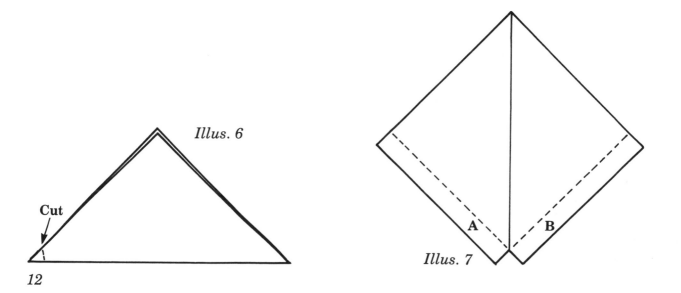

Illus. 6

Cut

Illus. 7

A   B

square over and place it on top of the larger square, so that the flaps point down, as seen in Illus. 8.

Fold flaps A and B under the edges of the larger square. You made flaps A and B when you folded the sides of the smaller square.

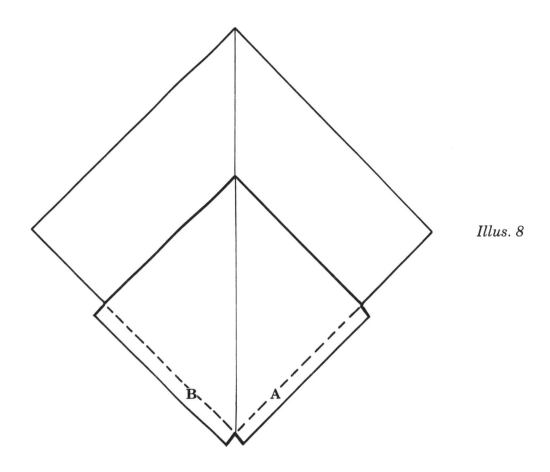

Illus. 8

Illus. 9 shows the rear view of the popper after the flaps are folded under. Use two strips of cellophane tape (as shown in the drawing) to fasten the two parts of the popper together. Glue will work as well as tape, but be sure to let the glue dry before you use your popper.

To make your popper pop, fold the larger square together. This means that the smaller square will fold right up inside the bigger one. Hold the heavier piece of material firmly between your thumb and finger. Be sure you hold the end opposite to the taped flaps. Make sure

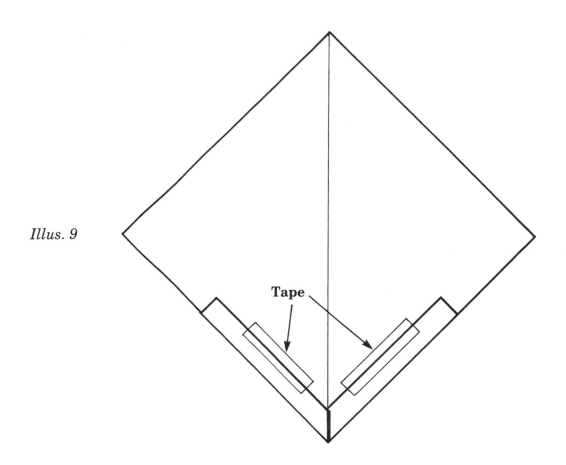

Illus. 9

Tape

that the folded edge of the larger square points up. Illus. 10 shows how things should look.

Snap your hand down quickly. If everything works properly, the smaller paper will unfold with a loud popping sound. If it doesn't unfold, try again. Make sure you snap down your hand hard and fast. If the popper still doesn't unfold and pop, make sure that the end of the popper you *aren't* holding can spread apart a bit to let the paper slip out. Sometimes the sides of the really stiff material don't spread the first few times.

After the toy pops, just fold the smaller square back into place, and then pop it again—and again, and again, and again!

Once you have the hang of it, there's nothing more fun than making all sorts of noise with your tricky *Two-Piece Paper Popper*.

After you pop it a number of times, the small paper will probably rip. When that happens, just peel the small paper off the heavy square and then fold and cut another

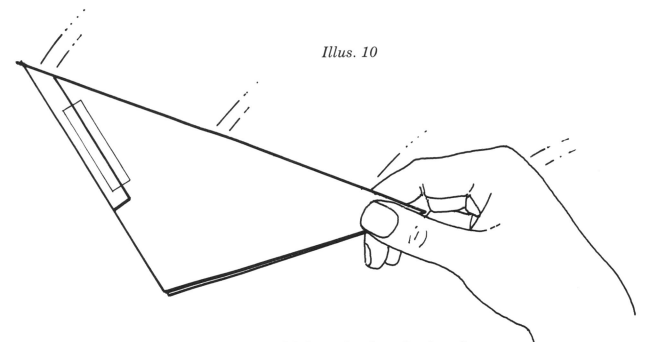

small square. Your popper should last for hundreds of loud pops.

Experiment with different-sized smaller squares. Try different types of paper. Make both squares larger and see how that works. When you find just the right size and type of paper, you'll really be in the popper business!

TRICKY CAMERA

This folded-paper trick isn't really a camera. Begin with a piece of paper twice as long as it is wide. A piece 10″ long and 5″ wide should be perfect. Place it on a table before you, as shown in Illus. 11. The dotted line in the drawing shows where you're going to make a fold. Fold the top down towards the bottom, so that the paper is now folded exactly in half. Leave the paper folded, so that it looks like the drawing shown in Illus. 12.

Place the folded paper on a pad of newspaper, and use a pin, an awl, a sharp pencil, or a ballpoint pen to make the four holes shown in Illus. 12. Poke the holes all the way through both layers of the folded paper. You have the pad of newspaper under the paper so you don't poke your finger and you won't make holes in your desk or

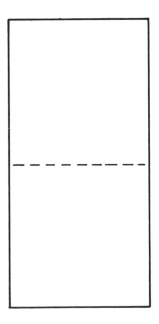

Illus. 11

Protect that tabletop!

table. Unfold the paper, and you're at the point shown in Illus. 13.

Now it's time for some scissors work. You're going to use the four holes you just poked as a guide to making some cuts. Look closely at the cut lines in Illus. 13 before you start cutting. Make three cuts in the top half and

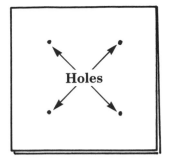

Illus. 12

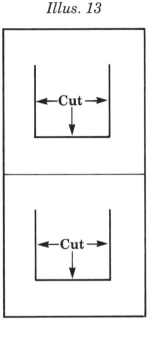

Illus. 13

another three cuts in the bottom half of the paper. Notice that the horizontal cut in each case is at the bottom of the two vertical cuts. This is important!

Use a ruler to guide your cutting and draw light lines to connect the guide holes. Then just cut along the lines. Carefully push the point of your scissors through the paper on one of the lines you just drew. Don't poke yourself with the scissors! One at a time, make all six cuts.

Once the cuts are made, the difficult part of making your *Tricky Camera* is over. Now all you need to do is a bit of artwork and you'll be ready to trick people.

Draw a face on the bottom flap. Check Illus. 14 to be sure that you're drawing on the right flap. Be sure the face is only on the flap—don't let it extend past the cuts.

Illus. 14

Illus. 15

17

Instead of drawing a face, you could cut out a face from an old magazine and glue it onto the flap. Use a movie star's face if you want to flatter the friends you'll "photograph" with your *Tricky Camera*. You might consider the face of a clown, a horse, a gorilla, or anything amusing.

Once you draw this face, draw the sides of a camera on either side of the face on the flap. You don't have to be an artist. Just make it look somewhat like a real camera. No one will ever think it's really a camera, anyway, so your artwork is just for effect. Things should now look somewhat like Illus. 15.

Now fold down the top half of the paper, and we're at Illus. 16. Draw a camera lens on the flap. Illus. 17 will give you some idea. Don't spend lots of time on the artwork unless you enjoy art.

Open up the paper again so it looks like it did in Illus. 15. Now fold the top half of the paper back and under along the fold line. When this is done, you'll be at Illus. 18.

It's almost photo time. Slip the lens flap through the opening below the funny face. Once this is done, your *Tricky Camera* will look like Illus. 19.

To take a "photo," open the bottom of the folded paper just enough so that the flap with the lens slips back and under. What's left is the funny face or the movie star's picture, or whatever you had in Illus. 18.

Look into the lens and take your own picture, just to see how the camera works. Practise the "quick flip" (with

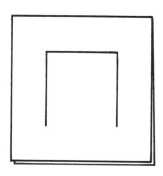

Illus. 16

Illus. 17

Illus. 18

Illus. 19

the camera pointed away from you) a few times so you can do it easily and smoothly when you want to take a trick photo of someone.

If you have a movie star's picture inside the camera, people will be flattered, although you've just used a piece of folded paper to trick them. Most people will laugh at a clown or other funny face. Don't use a picture that might hurt someone's feelings. It's one thing to play a trick and get a laugh. It's not fun to upset someone. Professional photographers sometimes get their cameras broken by unhappy subjects!

SNAP AND POP

Folded-paper noisemakers are lots of fun, but don't use them to drive other people crazy. This paper noisemaker can be made in just a minute. Use it to make lots and lots of great noise.

Begin with two sheets of notebook paper. Fold one sheet along the dotted line, as shown in Illus. 20. Make this fold about 1″ from the edge of the paper.

Fold the paper over and over so that you end up with a strip of paper about 1″ wide and eight layers thick. Use

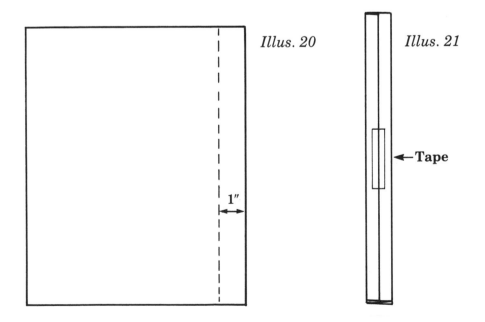

Illus. 20

Illus. 21

1″

←Tape

a bit of tape (as shown in Illus. 21) to keep the paper from unfolding.

Fold the second sheet of paper just as you did the first. If it's just a bit wider or narrower than the first sheet, don't worry. It won't hurt your toy in the least.

Place the two strips end-to-end so that they overlap about 1″. Illus. 22 shows this step. Use a strip of tape to fasten the two paper strips together. Place the tape over the loose end of the top strip and wrap the tape around both paper strips several times. Use either masking tape or cellophane tape. Check Illus. 23 to see how the two strips look when they're taped together.

Illus. 22

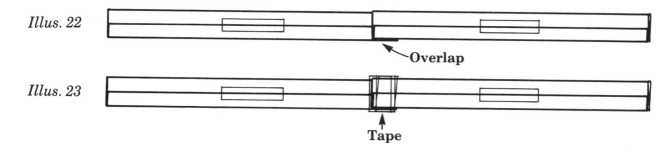

—Overlap

Illus. 23

Tape

For this toy to make wonderful noise, fold it in the middle, where you just taped it. Grasp the taped end between the thumb and fingers of one hand. Grip the loose ends firmly with the other hand in the same manner. Push your hands together so that a loop forms between the two layers of paper. Illus. 24 shows this step.

Pull your hands apart hard and fast. The arrows shown in Illus. 24 show the directions to move your hands. This pulling causes the loop between the layers of paper to close up, and both strips of paper will come

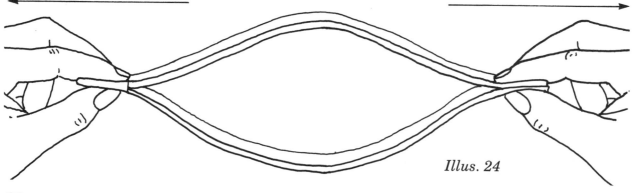

Illus. 24

together sharply. As the two layers of paper strike each other, you'll get a loud popping sound, if you let the hand holding the loose ends slide off the paper. This allows the paper to vibrate just a bit and to create a loud pop.

Practise this a few times until you see just how hard to pull your hands apart and just how to release the loose ends of the paper strips to get the loudest pop.

Make your next *Snap and Pop* toy using the tough paper from a large grocery bag. Since these bags are large, cut a sheet of paper 8″ or 9″ wide and long enough so that you don't have to join two smaller strips together.

Experiment by making these noisemakers a bit wider than 1″ and see whether they pop louder than the narrower ones.

COOTIE CATCHER

You've probably seen these around but didn't know how to make one. Now's the time to learn.

Begin with a sheet of notebook paper or typing paper. Since the paper must be square, learn how to turn a piece of rectangular notebook paper into a square. Fold one bottom corner over so that your paper looks like the drawing shown in Illus. 25. Cut off the shaded area seen in the drawing.

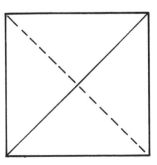

Illus. 25

Unfold the paper and you have a perfect square. Remember how to do this, because you'll often need a square piece of paper.

You made one diagonal fold in your paper when you first made it into a square. That fold is seen in Illus. 26. The dotted line in the drawing indicates the fold you'll make now. Fold the paper to form this diagonal and then unfold it. Where the two diagonal folds cross is the middle of the paper, shown by the arrow in Illus. 27.

Now fold all four corners of the paper so that each corner exactly touches the middle of the paper. The four dotted lines shown in Illus. 27 indicate these folds.

Once these folds are made, things should look like the drawing in Illus. 28. Turn the paper over and it should look like Illus. 29.

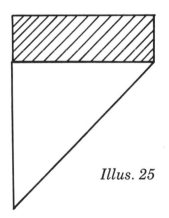

Illus. 26

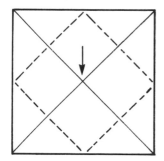 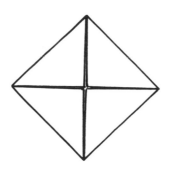 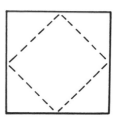

Illus. 27   *Illus. 28*   *Illus. 29*

There are four dotted lines in Illus. 29 to show where you'll make your next folds. Fold each corner into the middle again.

Once the corners are folded to the middle, your project is shown in Illus. 30. Draw some cooties for the catcher to catch. They're shown in Illus. 31.

Before you draw these pesky little cooties, take a close look at the illustration. The cooties only appear on two of

Eeww! Cooties!

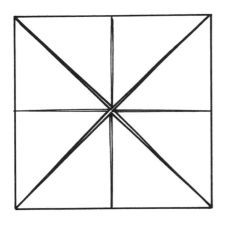

Illus. 30

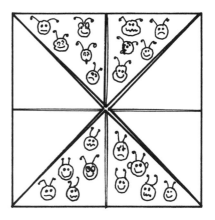

Illus. 31

the little triangular folds of paper. (A cootie can be drawn any way you like.)

Once you've drawn a few cooties, turn the paper over. It looks like Illus. 32. To finish your *Cootie Catcher*, open it up so that your thumb and three fingers fit inside to operate it.

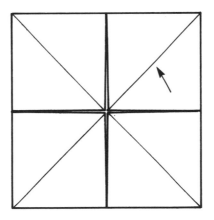

Illus. 32

Lift up on the fold shown by the arrow in Illus. 32. As you bend the paper back along the fold, it forms a little pocket as that corner of the catcher opens.

Do the same for the other three corners of the project. You'll probably find it helps to coax all four corners open at once. When the catcher is fully open and ready for use, it looks like Illus. 33.

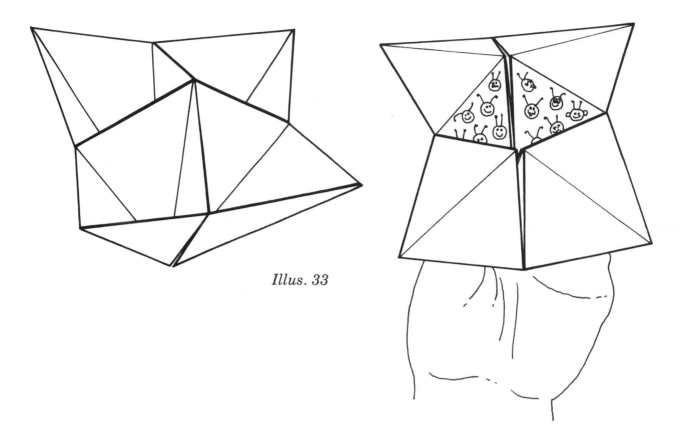

Illus. 33

Insert your thumb into one of the open sections and one finger into each of the other parts. Your little finger can fit in with your fourth finger, or let it stick out into space. That's up to you. Your fingers don't have to go all the way into the points.

Now, by opening and closing your fingers, the opposite sides of the catcher turn into four little jaws. Work with it for just a minute and you'll discover that when you work the jaws one way all you see is paper. Work them from the other side and all those horrid little cooties you drew appear.

Get the coordination right and the catcher should work beautifully.

Here's what your grandfather did next. He approached someone, usually a girl he wanted to impress, and opened the catcher wide, with only the plain inner jaws showing.

Then he worked the jaws as though catching something on the girl's arm, back, hair, or whatever. Then he opened the catcher so the sides with the cooties were open.

At this point he exclaimed, "Look! Cooties!"

Of course you risk upsetting someone if you pull this trick, but perhaps you like to live dangerously. You could use your *Cootie Catcher* just to pick up small objects.

IT FLOATS!

Most people know that you can fold a sheet of typing paper to make a little boat, and that it will float. It's a fun project you should try.

However, when you tell people you're going to float a flat sheet of paper in a sink full of water, they often suspect that you're about to trick them. Which you are, of course.

Before you perform this wonderful floating paper trick, cut a sheet of cereal box cardboard about 4″ wide by 6″ long. It doesn't have to be exactly that size, but come close. You'll also need a sheet of typing paper.

Now fill the kitchen sink half-full of water and wait for any waves or ripples to subside.

Check your sheet of typing paper to make sure that none of the edges or the corners are bent downwards. This is important! If the edges turn up a bit, that's fine.

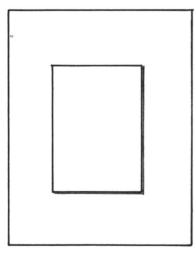

Illus. 34

Illus. 35

They just shouldn't turn down! Use your fingers to be sure that all four edges have a slight upward bend, if you wish.

Carefully set the paper on the water. It floats! Now place the little rectangle of cereal-box cardboard right in the middle of the floating paper. Ease it onto the paper. Don't *drop* it on the paper. The project should look like Illus. 34 at this point.

Now comes the real trick. Place a coin or a button (or something that doesn't roll) on the cardboard. Put it right in the middle, because you have to keep the entire project balanced, Does the coin's weight sink the floating paper? No way.

Add a few more coins, buttons, erasers, pencils, or other objects. Make certain that you have as much weight on one side of the sheet of the cardboard as you have on the other. Don't pile things up at one end or on one edge, because then the paper will become unbalanced, and it will sink.

Illus. 35 shows objects in balance, and Illus. 36 shows you what *not* to do, just in case there's any question.

Illus. 36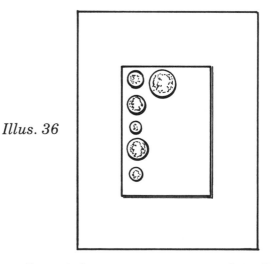

How much weight can you put on this floating sheet of paper? The only way to find out is to try for yourself. The paper can hold several forks or spoons without sinking, if you want to start with silverware instead of coins.

This is a great paper trick to amaze others or to use at parties. Practise it first, so you know what to expect, then go out and surprise people!

FOLDED-PAPER MAGIC

There's nothing greater than performing a bit of magic that leaves others wondering exactly how you worked a trick. In this chapter, you'll learn how to turn folded paper into surprising magic tricks.

These magic tricks don't need hours and hours of practice in order for them to work; they'll work for you the first time you try them! Always remember this about these magic tricks and any other folded paper tricks: Check them out on your own. Never, never, try to "go public" until you've worked on the trick by yourself, and you're absolutely certain that you understand how to make it work. With that in mind, let's learn some great tricks.

WHO'S ON TOP?

This great little trick doesn't use folded paper, it uses *rolled* paper. This trick is so amazing that no one will argue about whether your paper is folded or rolled.

Begin with two pieces of paper, both exactly the same size. A good size is 4″ by 7″. Although the papers are the same size, they should be different colors. Cut both pieces from regular typing paper and color one piece with a crayon or a felt-tipped marker. If you have paper of different colors handy, use that. Arrange the two pieces of paper as shown in Illus. 37.

Make a mental note of which piece of paper is now on top. If necessary, make a written note!

Begin slowly, carefully, rolling the two pieces of paper starting at the point shown by the arrow in Illus. 37. Keep the roll fairly tight, so that it's about ⅜″ in diameter. Don't roll it so tight that you crease the paper. As you roll the two pieces of paper, let the left side of the roll get a little larger than the right side; you'll see why in just a minute.

Illus. 38 shows how things look after you've started rolling the two papers.

Now, here comes the tricky part. See the arrow pointing to the corner of the paper at the upper left? *Keep your eye on that corner.* When that corner of paper goes around the roll one time, and one time *only*, stop rolling instantly. The second the top corner of the left paper comes around the roll and falls back onto the table, it's time to stop rolling.

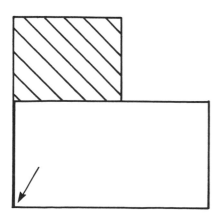

Illus. 37

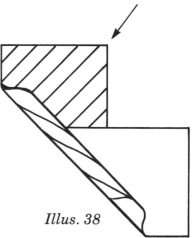

Illus. 38

If you let the left side of the roll be just a little bigger than the right side, everything should be perfect at this point. Although the top corner of the left sheet of paper has come around the roll once, the corner at the right has not yet been rolled up. This is important for the trick to work.

Place a finger on the left corner you've been watching. Hold it down on the table so it can't get away. Remember to hold it down after that corner has come around the roll for the first time.

Now, slowly unroll the two papers. When you do this trick for someone else, have the spectator put one finger on each of the top corners, left and right, and have him hold them tightly onto the table.

Whether the corners are held to the table or not really doesn't matter. What *does* matter is that by having a spectator hold the corners down firmly, it makes the trick ever so much better.

When the two papers are unrolled, everyone should have a surprise coming. The papers should look like Illus. 39.

Now the paper on the left is on top. Check back to Illus. 37, which shows the paper at the right on top, as it was originally.

Practise this a few times, then go looking for someone to surprise. Just remember that the corner at the upper left has to come around once, and then you're in business.

Illus. 39

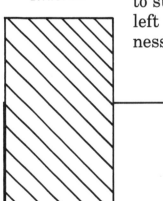

INVINCIBLE PAPER

Something *invincible* can't be overcome or beaten. You'll astound others with this tricky paper fold by showing them a piece of stiff paper or cardboard that's so powerful that neither a pencil point nor a pen point will go through it.

This folded-paper magic trick takes just a bit of preparation. Begin by folding a sheet of notebook paper or typing paper into an envelope. Fold the paper in half along the dotted line, as shown in Illus. 40.

Once the paper is folded, make the cut shown in Illus. 41. Cut only the *top* layer of paper. If you cut both layers, you'll end up with two pieces of paper and no envelope.

After making the cut in the top layer of paper, complete the envelope by running a strip of tape along the open side and the bottom. If you don't have tape, use glue. Run only a thin line of glue along the edges of the paper. Don't tape or glue the top; it has to stay open so you can slip your *Invincible Paper* inside.

Now cut the "invincible" paper. Stiff paper or even cereal-box cardboard is best, since you have to be able to slide the paper easily into the envelope. However, notebook paper will also work—you just have to be more careful when you perform the trick.

The envelope you just made is about 5½″ by 8½″. Cut your "invincible" piece of paper just slightly smaller than the envelope. If you glued the edges, remember that the inside of the envelope is smaller than the outside.

Slip this piece of material into the envelope just to be sure it fits without a lot of pushing and pulling.

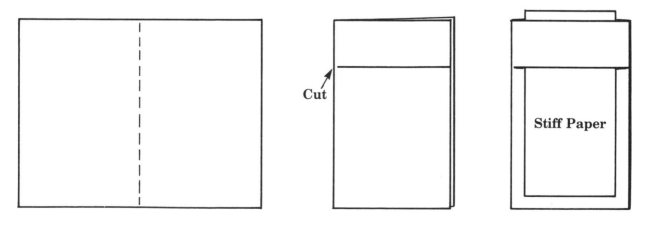

Illus. 40   Illus. 41   Illus. 42

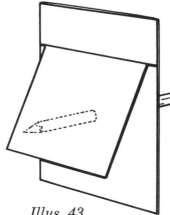

Now to perform your folded-paper trick! What you seem to do is to slip the stiff piece of material into the envelope and then poke a pencil or pen all the way through the envelope. But what's the trick?

The trick: Once the pencil is all the way through the envelope, you'll pull the stiff sheet of paper or cardboard out of the envelope. Not only won't it have a hole in it, but the pencil will still be sticking through the envelope.

Here's how this trick works. When you slip the stiff sheet into the envelope, you only start sliding it in at the top. The bottom of the sheet goes out through the slit you cut, so that the bottom part of the *Invincible Paper* is never inside the envelope at all. Check Illus. 42 to see how this works.

When you perform this folded-paper trick, make sure that all your audience sees is the *front* of the envelope. If someone sees the back, with the cardboard sticking out of the slot, then the trick's over and the joke will be on you.

As you can see in Illus. 43, when you push the pencil or pen through the envelope, it goes through both sides of the envelope, but it doesn't go through the "invincible" part. Push the pencil through the envelope so that it points down to help it slide along the "invincible" paper that you don't want harmed.

Illus. 43

"HELP!"

Don't let this happen to you! Practice makes perfect!

Push the pencil through the envelope at a point lower than the slot. Otherwise, you'll spoil the trick and your *Invincible Paper* as well.

Perform this trick with a bit of polish. When you push the pencil through the envelope, be careful not to push it through your hand. Be sure to hold the envelope *above* the slot. This will keep your hand out of danger, and it also lets the stiff paper or cardboard slide *up* as the pencil comes through the envelope.

Make a little production of this. Pretend you're pushing quite hard in order to go through the material inside. Don't overdo it, but make it look good.

Hold up the envelope so that your audience sees just the front. Push the pencil into the envelope at least half the pencil's length. Wiggle it around just a bit.

Then, with the pencil still poked through the envelope, pull the stiff sheet out. You could even let the audience see the pencil sticking out of the back of the envelope. Do this in such a way that they can't see the slot you cut.

Practise this a few times to make certain that you can perform it without letting anyone see the back of the envelope. Then try it on a friend or two.

The next time you entertain young children, you'll find that they think that this trick is really special.

ANTI-GRAVITY PAPER

Gravity works on all things. Otherwise, when you drop a pencil or an eraser, it might just go drifting off into space instead of falling to the floor. One thing *does* defy the laws of gravity—the *Anti-Gravity Paper* you're about to make.

Begin with a sheet of notebook paper or typing paper. Fold it along the dotted line, as shown in Illus. 44. Fold the bottom edge up at least ½", but not more than ¾".

Once this fold is in place, your paper should look like Illus. 45. The dotted lines in the drawing indicate the next folds you'll be making. Just fold over the paper

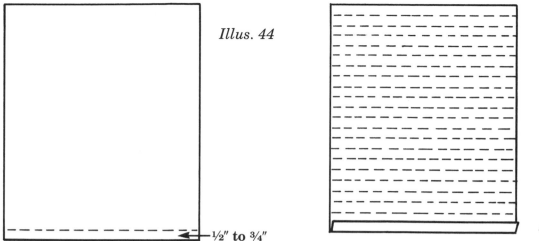

Illus. 44

Illus. 45

½″ to ¾″

again and again so that the first fold is inside the many folds you make.

Once the entire sheet of paper is folded into a long, narrow strip, use a couple of strips of tape to hold the loose edge in place. The drawing in Illus. 46 shows the tape in place.

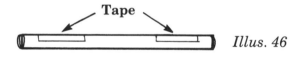

Tape

Illus. 46

That's all you need to do to make your *Anti-Gravity Paper!* Now it's up to your skill as a performer to make this folded-paper trick work. Work with a little polish and you'll impress everyone who sees you perform this trick.

Begin by holding the paper in your hand as shown in Illus. 47. It doesn't matter whether you hold the paper in your right hand or your left hand. But you should *always* hold your wrist with your other hand. You want your audience to get used to seeing one hand around the other wrist.

When you turn over the hand holding the paper, it shouldn't surprise anyone that the paper remains where it is. After all, everyone can see your thumb holding the paper in place, as shown in Illus. 48.

The surprise comes when you slip your thumb out from under the paper and the paper still remains in place.

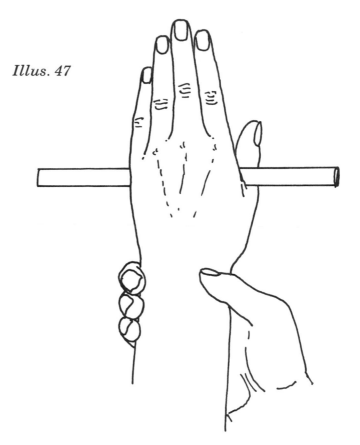

The *Anti-Gravity Paper* doesn't fall because the index finger of your other hand holds the paper pressed into your palm.

Illus. 49 shows how this works. The dotted line shows your index finger—it's hidden from the audience's view. It better be hidden, or there goes your folded-paper trick!

To make this trick work well, give your audience a buildup. Here's one way to do this: Begin by mentioning that gravity pulls things towards the center of the Earth. Say something about the special *Anti-Gravity Paper* in your hand.

When you turn your hand over, mention that gravity is exerting a real pull. In fact, it's pulling so hard on the paper, that you must use both hands to keep it from falling.

Let your hand steady. Tell the audience that your *Anti-Gravity Paper* is working. Pull away the thumb that's holding the paper, but don't hold the paper with

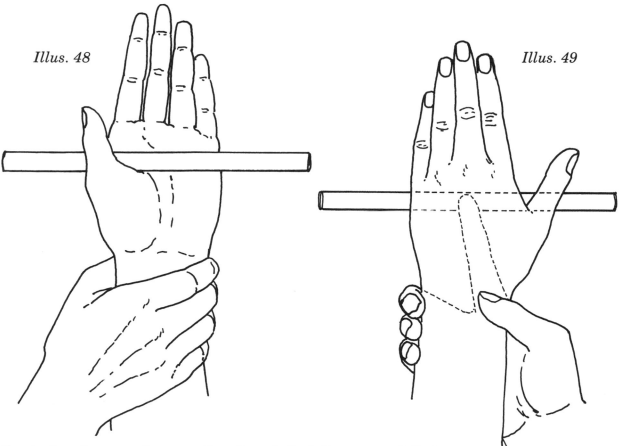

the index finger of your other hand. Let the paper fall, to get a good laugh, even if it is at your expense.

Act puzzled, pick up the paper again so that your hands and the paper look as they did in Illus. 47. Now turn your hands over again.

This time, when you move your thumb away, slip the other index finger up and press the paper into place. Now, when your thumb comes away, the paper stays in place. Look pleased, take a bow, but *never* tell how you made this trick work.

If you want to make this trick last longer, push on the sides of the folded paper so that the center opens up. Slip a pencil inside the folded paper. Say something about how the paper needs more weight in order to fall to the floor.

Of course, the paper won't fall—it can't with your finger holding it in place! By adding the pencil and repeating the trick, it distracts the audience—they won't wonder how you got the paper to stay in place.

SNAP AND CLIP

This truly amazing folded-paper trick really gets people's attention. You'll be bending the paper, or perhaps you'll be folding it, but without creasing it. Whether you bend it, or have a creaseless fold, you'll have a great time performing this fantastic trick.

You'll need a strip of tough paper about 8″ long by 3″ wide. The paper needs to be fairly tough because you're eventually going to give it a good snap, and you don't want it to rip. Notebook paper or typing paper will work fine; just don't snap the strip into two pieces. If that happens, just cut another strip of paper and start over.

To make your notebook paper stronger, cut a strip 8″ long by about 6″ wide. Then fold it in half along the dotted line, as shown in Illus. 50.

If you use folded paper, the fold should face *up* in the next steps.

Bend your paper into the shape of a flattened-out S.

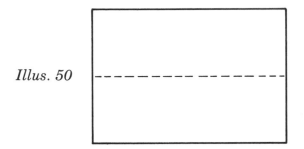

Illus. 50

Illus. 51 shows a top view of the paper once it's been bent into shape. You don't want to crease the bends or folds, because creasing weakens the paper and makes it more likely to tear when you eventually give it a snap.

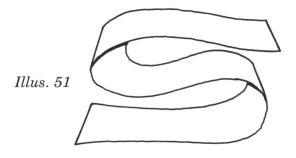

Illus. 51

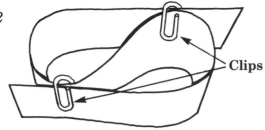

Illus. 53

Clips

Now slip two paper clips over the top of the paper, as shown in Illus. 52. Place the clips *exactly* as they're shown in the drawing.

Get a firm hold on the two loose ends of the paper. The arrows in Illus. 52 show where to grab if there is any question. Pull your hands apart with a quick snapping motion. Don't pull so hard that you rip the paper, but be sure that you pull quickly and firmly as you snap your hands apart.

The two paper clips should go flying off into space, so keep an eye on them. Make sure nothing vulnerable is in their path.

When you (or someone else if you're performing this trick) picks up the paper clips, be ready for a surprise. The two paper clips are now interlocked, as shown in Illus. 53.

Practise this a few times, to determine exactly how hard you have to snap your hands apart.

Let's move on to bigger and better things. Take a quick look at the next drawing shown in Illus. 54. This time there are *three* paper clips in place.

Bend the paper, slip the clips onto the paper, and snap your hands apart again. When you gather up the three clips, they should all be joined together.

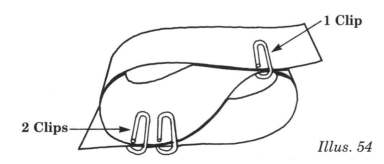

1 Clip

2 Clips

Illus. 54

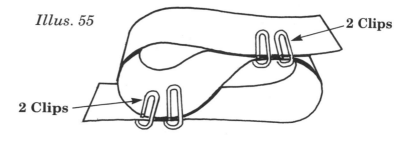

Illus. 55

2 Clips

2 Clips

Illus. 56

Move on to even bigger tricks. Set up your paper with *four* paper clips, like the one shown in Illus. 55.

When you try three or four clips, it may help if you make your strip of paper longer than 8″. Cut a strip from a piece of typing paper the long way, and it will be 11″ long, giving you more room for bends and clips.

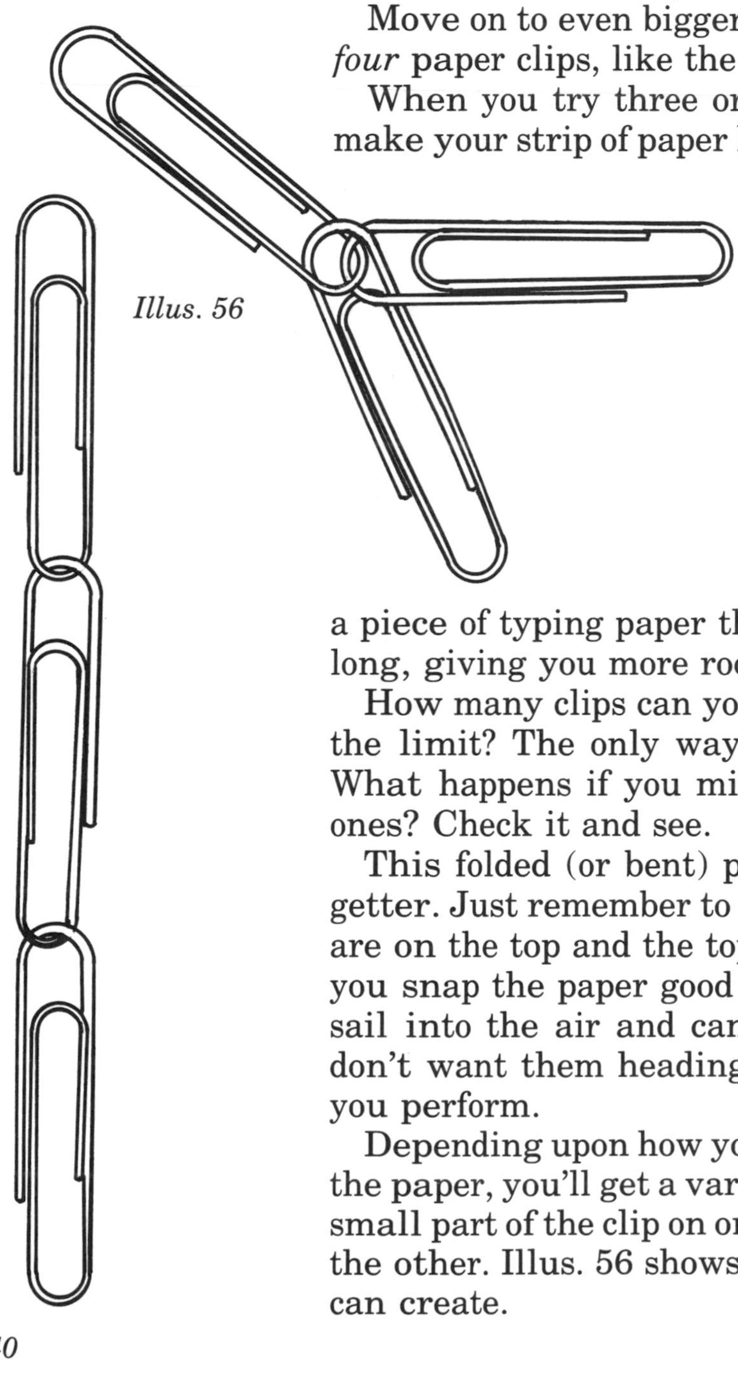

How many clips can you entangle in this way? Is four the limit? The only way to find out is to experiment. What happens if you mix larger clips in with smaller ones? Check it and see.

This folded (or bent) paper trick is a real attention-getter. Just remember to hold the paper so that the clips are on the top and the top is pointed straight up. When you snap the paper good and hard, the paper clips will sail into the air and can travel quite a distance. You don't want them heading right at the people watching you perform.

Depending upon how you slip the clips over the edge of the paper, you'll get a variety of linkups. Try putting the small part of the clip on one side of the paper and then on the other. Illus. 56 shows a few of the combinations you can create.

Protect your eyes from flying paper clips!

UNCUTTABLE PAPER

This folded-paper trick takes just a minute to prepare, and it leaves your audience wondering just how you did what they saw you do.

Begin by making an envelope using a sheet of notebook paper or typing paper. This envelope is open at both ends, because you're going to slip a strip of stiff paper or light cardboard through it. The two dotted lines shown in Illus. 57 indicate where you're going to fold the sheet of paper to form this envelope.

Making the envelope is simple. Just fold up the bottom of the paper, as indicated by the lower dotted line. Then fold down the top, so it becomes a flap. Use a bit of glue or a strip of tape to hold the flap down and your "magic" envelope is assembled!

Now comes the tricky part. For your magic trick to be a success, you have to cut a slit in the back of the envelope, as shown in Illus. 58.

Illus. 57

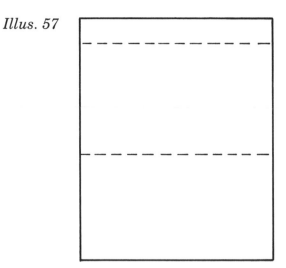

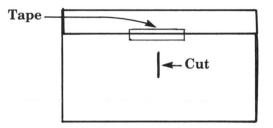

Illus. 58

Cut this slit through the back of the envelope only. If your scissors go through the front (the part your audience will see), the trick is over before it began, and the laugh will be on you.

The slit you cut in the back of the envelope should be about 1″ long. Be careful when you poke the point of the scissors through the paper—don't pierce the front of the envelope or poke your finger.

Set the envelope aside for a minute. Now it's time to cut the amazing *magic* strip of stiff paper or cardboard.

Cut a strip of material a little less than 1″ wide and about 12″ long. To improve the way this trick looks, color one side of the strip, if you're using file-folder material or other stiff material that's not fairly bright. If you're using a piece of cereal-box cardboard, one side is already colored, so you're ahead of the game.

Now for the trick itself. Slip the strip of material you just cut through the envelope. This is simple, because both ends of the envelope are open. Turn the colored side of the strip away from you so your audience can see the ends of the strip easily. Illus. 59 shows things at this point.

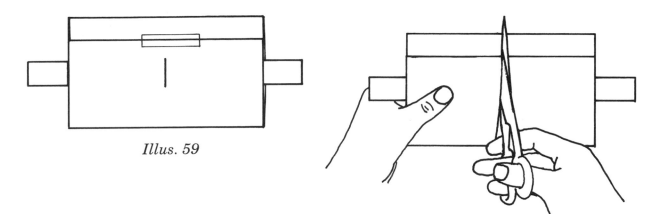

Notice that the strip is pushed *through* the envelope, so it passes right *under* the slit you cut. This is very important!

Pick up your scissors. Tell your audience that now you're going to cut the envelope into two pieces because you need two small envelopes and two shorter strips of colored material.

Begin cutting from the bottom upwards. Hold the envelope firmly in the hand that isn't holding the scissors. Make sure you hold the envelope so that you have a good grip on the strip inside. You don't want the strip to slip away from its place under the slit in the back of the envelope.

Cut very slowly. Tell your audience that you have to be careful to cut a perfectly straight line. Of course, you're cutting slowly because you don't want any problems when you get to the strip of cardboard that you're *not* going to cut.

When you reach the slit in the back of the envelope, it's time to work your magic. Make certain that the tip of your scissors slips *under* the cardboard. Slip your scissors *under* the cardboard and keep on cutting slowly. Just follow the path of the slit you cut when you made the envelope, and everything will turn out well.

Now you're only cutting the front of the envelope. Those watching have no way of knowing that you aren't cutting both sides of the envelope. Illus. 60 shows your scissor work once you've passed under the strip of cardboard.

Once you snip your way past the cardboard strip, the point of your scissors must now come up from beneath the cardboard, so you cut both sides of the envelope, just as you did when you started at the bottom.

Finish cutting. Say that now you have two envelopes and two little strips of cardboard, so you can get on with your trick. Pull the two parts of the envelope apart and then pretend to look surprised.

Say, "Look at that! That cardboard strip didn't get cut. Now how did that happen?" Slide the two halves of cut envelope back and forth on the strip as shown in Illus. 61.

Illus. 61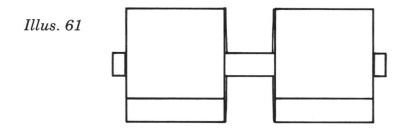

Someone will want you to remove the envelope pieces. Do so. Someone will ask to check the cardboard strip. Let it be checked—it's perfect. Say, "The same thing happened to me the last time I did this trick."

This trick is really difficult for an audience to accept. They watched as you pushed the cardboard strip through the envelope. Both ends of the strip stuck out from the sides of the envelope. They saw you cut the envelope into two pieces. Now the strip is *whole*. It's truly puzzling!

Be sure you practise this folded-paper trick a few times before you go public. It's not all that difficult to slip the scissor tip under the cardboard, but it does take some careful movement with your scissors. Like all good things, practise makes perfect.

MOVING PAPER

Let's work on another paper trick. Here the paper is rolled, instead of creased and folded. You need three square pieces of paper. Notebook paper is just fine. Each piece should be about 8″ square. If you don't remember

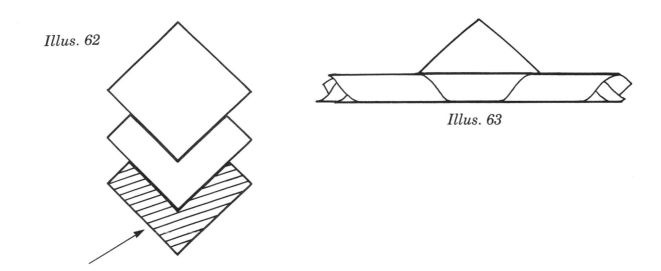

Illus. 62

Illus. 63

how to turn a rectangular sheet of paper into a square, glance back to page 21.

Color one of the squares on both sides. If you have colored paper handy, use it. Or, use lined notebook paper for two squares and plain white paper for the third.

Place the three squares on the table before you so that they're arranged as shown in Illus. 62.

Roll the squares into a ½″-diameter tube. Start rolling at the bottom of the line of squares. This means you begin to roll the colored square. The arrow in the drawing shows where you'll begin to roll.

When you're about halfway done rolling the paper squares into a tube, your paper trick should look like Illus. 63.

Keep rolling slowly. The point of one of the squares will finally come around the rolled tube. It will flip over the tube and be in front of you for just an instant. The second square's corner will follow.

This is important. As soon as the second point flips over, begin unrolling the squares. Reverse the direction you're rolling the papers, and then go backwards. Illus. 64 shows what you'll see when you finish unrolling the three squares.

The squares probably won't be quite as neatly arranged as those shown in the drawing, but the colored square will now be between the two plain ones.

Illus. 64

Even up the papers so that they look like Illus. 64 and they're spaced nicely. Repeat the rolling procedure exactly as before. Let two corners come around and flip down, then unroll the tube.

This time the squares will be in the position shown in Illus. 65. By now you should have everyone's attention.

Even up the squares, as you did before. This time, roll them forward, but let only *one* corner flip over, and then unroll them. Instead of telling you what you'll see, find out for yourself!

Once you've unrolled the squares, and seen where the colored square is now, repeat the process again, with only one corner flipping down before unrolling.

When you're ready to perform this paper trick for your friends, just remember this little rule: Two flips move up. One flip moves down. That way you'll always know where to expect the colored square to appear.

Try letting *three* corners flip over before unrolling, and see what difference that makes in the arrangement.

After you've practised this trick a few times, and you're sure you know where the colored square will appear, you can make it appear anywhere you want. Work up a routine, and you've got a fantastic paper trick to use over and over.

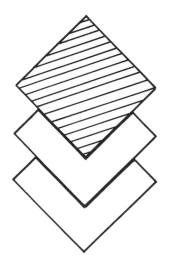

Illus. 65

A FEW FOLDS AND A CUT OR TWO

Some of the greatest folded-paper tricks require only a few folds and a cut or two. There may be occasions when you'll need a special greeting card that contains a surprise. You'll learn how to make several in this chapter.

It always surprises young children when you fold a strip of paper, make a few cuts, and unfold it to show that you've just made a chain of identical figures. Even better, the chain can be used for decoration.

Paper loops contain lots of surprises most people have never dreamed of. Now's the time for you to learn about them.

The next time you need to cut out a perfect star without spending lots of time measuring and hoping for the best, you'll be able to. Just a few folds and a couple of quick cuts and you'll turn out perfect figures.

POP-UP FOLDED-CARD SURPRISES

Everyone enjoys opening a greeting card and having a figure pop up! Now's the time to learn how to make several different types of these great greeting cards.

This first pop-up card unfolds itself from the middle of the card as it's opened. This card is made from two identically-sized pieces of paper.

Decide how large you want your card to be and cut two pieces of paper twice that size. Make the first card out of material the size of a sheet of typing paper ($8\frac{1}{2}'' \times 11''$). Now you won't have to worry about cutting paper to a certain size. After you've made your first card of this type, experiment with cards of any size. Begin by folding both sheets of paper in half. The dotted line in Illus. 66 shows this fold. Set one folded paper aside. You'll get to it in a minute.

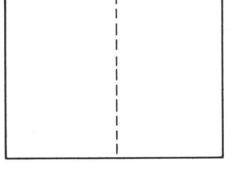

Illus. 66

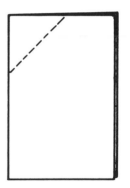

Illus. 67

While the second sheet is still folded double, fold it along the dotted line, as shown in Illus. 67. Be sure you fold *along* the fold. Illus. 68 shows how things look after making this fold.

Fold the paper backwards along the fold line you just made, making the folds good and limber so they'll fold in either direction.

Now flatten out this fold and it looks just as it did in Illus. 67, except that the dotted line is now a fold line.

Draw half of the figure you wish to have pop up when the card is opened. Illus. 69 gives you four ideas for this card. The heart could be for Valentine's Day, and the egg is perfect for an Easter card. The Christmas tree and the snowman are great for the winter holidays.

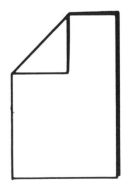

Illus. 68

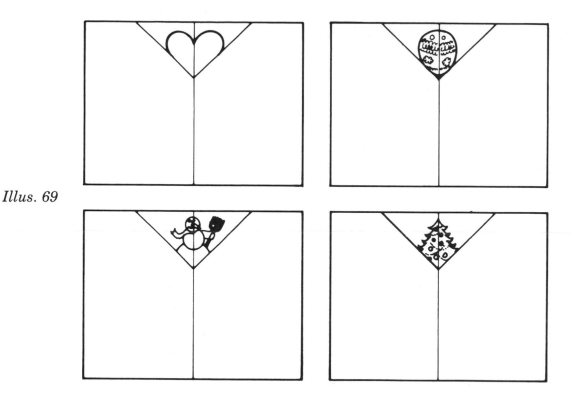

Illus. 69

Illus. 70

Note that there's a bit of space at the top of each figure. This leaves a band of paper joining both sides of the card. This is important.

Make sure you don't draw any lines extending past the fold you just made. This is important, too. Now, with the card still folded, cut along the lines you just drew. Try the heart first, because it's the easiest to cut.

Once you've cut out the top of the heart, unfold the paper and lift up. Illus. 70 shows this step. The pop-up heart should fold up *inside* the card when the card is closed. When the card opens, the heart pops right up.

Now's a good time to decorate the card. Color the pop-up heart red or pink. Add some other little hearts here and there on the card. Maybe you'll write a short message, as well.

After the decorating is finished, it's time to put the card together. Now you'll need the second folded sheet you set aside earlier.

Put a bit of glue on the back of the decorated card so you can glue it inside the other section. *Don't* let any glue get onto the heart; it's going to unfold when the card is opened. Put just a tiny bit of glue on the band of

50

paper above the heart, so that it gets glued down, along with the rest of the inner portion of the card.

Illus. 71 shows how the two parts of the card look just as you're about to glue them together. You can see the glue on the inside section.

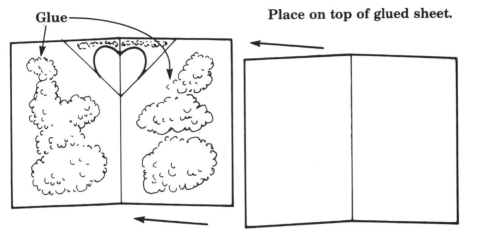

The two parts of the card should overlap exactly, and the middle folds should also match. Smooth the card and let it dry for a minute or so. Then you can write a message inside, or add some hearts to the outside of the card.

With this design and any other, remember not to cut past the angled fold, and remember to leave a band of paper at the top.

Use just a little bit of glue!

When you fold your card, use one finger to pull the heart or the snowman (or whatever) forward, so that when the card is closed the pop-up figure is turned inside out. The figure will stick down inside the folded card. When the card opens, the figure unfolds, which is what causes it to pop up and out at the card's recipient.

Feel free to make the inside fold (that's the one from Illus. 67 and Illus. 68) larger or smaller than the one you just made. The only way to determine how large or how small you want the pop-up fold to be is to try different sizes.

Another great way to make an interesting pop-up greeting card is to glue a figure you've cut from a magazine (or other source) onto the inner fold. For Christmas you might attach a reindeer and for Halloween you might want to paste a pumpkin onto the pop-up fold. Illus. 72 shows how such a figure looks when attached to the inside of your card.

Make sure that your reindeer or other figure doesn't extend past the diagonal folds that allow it to pop out when the card is opened. Check Illus. 72 to see that the figure doesn't extend past the fold lines.

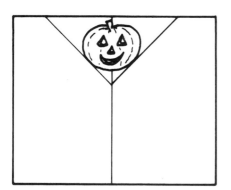

Illus. 72   *Illus. 73*

Illus. 73 shows another tricky way to glue a design or figure onto the middle of the card. Apply glue only to the paper on one side of the middle fold. The dotted line shows where the glue is beneath the figure.

Once the card is folded, the entire figure is hidden inside. When the card is opened, the inside design not only pops up, it can even stick up above the top of the card, or to one side of the card. Try this for yourself to see just how it works, and to see how large an inside figure you can use without having it stick out of the card once it's folded.

Illus. 74

You could also write a message on the pop-up fold so that the message catches the attention of the card's recipient. Illus. 74 shows how this can be done to make a tricky greeting card.

Once you've made a few cards like these, it's time to make a different kind of pop-up card.

You've probably made "cat steps" or "cat springs" before. Just in case you haven't, or you've forgotten how, take a minute to review how these little springs are made. One (or more) of them will help you make a tricky folded card.

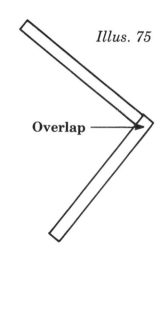

Illus. 75

Overlap

Begin with two strips of paper; they should both be the same width. They may be as long as you want, but for this first one, just cut two strips off the long side of a sheet of typing paper. Make each strip about ¾″ wide. If you want to get fancy, use paper strips of different colors.

Begin by placing the strips in the position shown in Illus. 75. Fasten the two strips together with a bit of glue or with a piece of cellophane tape. Now fold one strip over the other, so that the two strips look like Illus. 76.

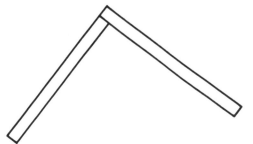

Illus. 76

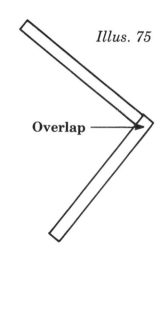

Illus. 77

53

Next, fold down the other strip over the one you just folded. Your spring should look like Illus. 77.

Keep folding one strip over the other until your spring is finished, and it will look like Illus. 78. Fasten the loose ends at the top using glue or tape.

Illus. 78

You can quite easily make a spring longer than this one. Cut two more strips of paper and fasten them to the ends of the first strips before you end the spring, as you did in Illus. 78. You don't want to fasten two or three or more strips of paper together (to begin with) because you'll get extremely long strips, and they're a real problem when you fold them back and forth over each other.

Now that the spring is finished, let's see how to use it in a tricky comic greeting card. Write *I told you not to open this!* on a small slip of paper or on a card about 2″ square.

Glue this card to the top of your cat spring. While the glue dries, fold your greeting card and write DO NOT OPEN! on the outside, as shown in Illus. 79.

Open the card and glue the bottom of the spring to the inside of the card. Things should now look like Illus. 80.

By now you should know how this tricky folded card works. Test it yourself, just to see it in action.

Illus. 79

Illus. 80

Another way to use these springs to make a terrific card is shown in Illus. 81. The clown's nose is mounted on a spring, and the nose pops out when the card is opened. The red spots on the clown's cheeks are also on springs and they come popping up at the same time, when the card is opened.

Naturally, you've written HAPPY BIRTHDAY! or COME TO A PARTY or some other greeting on the outside of the card.

In Illus. 82, all four of the bear's paws pop out when the card is opened. This is lots of fun for younger children, who will open and close the card time after time just to see the paws pop out at them.

Another way to use this cat spring is shown in Illus. 83 and Illus. 84. The spring has to be long enough so that both ends touch the paper at the same time, as the spring forms a half circle. Test your spring to make certain that it's long enough before you glue it onto the card. Glance

Illus. 81

Illus. 82

ahead to Illus. 85 to see how the spring looks when it's in place.

Place a little dab of glue on one end of the spring. Glue that end down as shown in Illus. 83. Now put a bit of glue on top of the spring and close the card on it, as seen in Illus. 84. Once the glue sets, open the card, and the spring should form a half circle, like the one shown in Illus. 85.

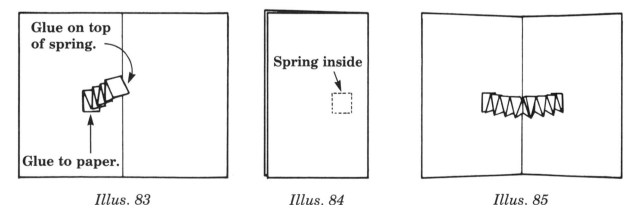

Illus. 83 *Illus. 84* *Illus. 85*

If you use orange paper to make the cat spring, draw the rest of a Halloween pumpkin around it, and you'll have a fine greeting card or a party invitation.

Place the spring near the top of the card to form a crown for a birthday card, or for a friendship card. A cat spring like this also makes a great middle for an Easter egg.

Illus. 86

Illus. 86 shows two of these ideas. You probably have many more ideas for using cat springs in tricky greeting cards.

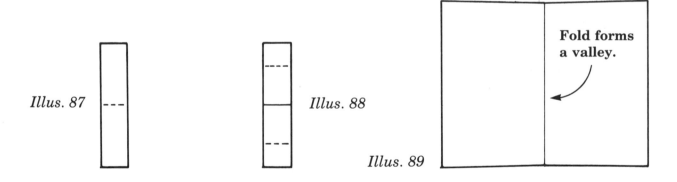

Illus. 87

Illus. 88

Fold forms a valley.

Illus. 89

Here's one more quick way to turn folded paper into a great pop-up greeting card. Begin by cutting a strip of fairly stiff paper 2″ wide (or a bit less) and 6″ long. Fold it in the middle, as shown by the dotted line in Illus. 87.

Once you've made this fold, unfold the paper. Now make the two folds shown by the dotted lines in Illus. 88. Each of these folds should be about 1¼″ from the end of the paper.

With all three folds in place, turn over the strip of paper so that the folds look like little mountains. Now open your greeting card so that it lies flat, just like the card shown in Illus. 89.

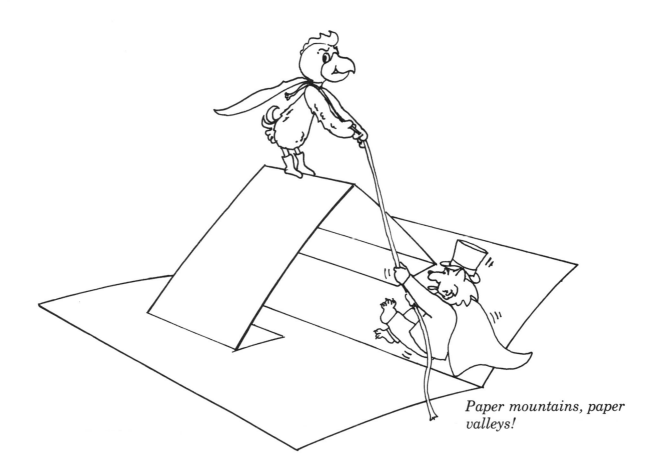

Paper mountains, paper valleys!

Run little lines of glue along both ends of the 2″ folded strip. Illus. 90 shows how. Fold under the two glued ends of the strip, and carefully place the strip on top of the card so that things look just like Illus. 91.

Make absolutely certain that the middle fold in the strip is directly above the fold in the greeting card. The fold in the card forms a little valley and the fold in the 2″ strip forms a little ridge.

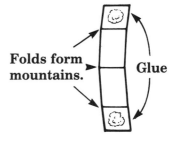

Folds form mountains. **Glue**

Illus. 90

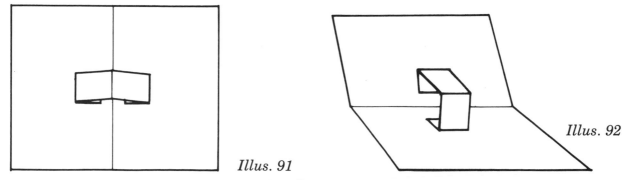

Illus. 91

Illus. 92

Carefully press the two glued ends of the strip onto the card. There's a space between these ends and the middle fold of the card. This is exactly the way it should be.

Once the glue dries and you open the card, the strip you just glued in place will rise, and it will look like the one shown in Illus. 92.

Now choose a figure you'd like to have stand up and pop out of the card when it's opened. Draw the figure yourself, or cut it from a magazine. Use fairly stiff paper for this one part of the project. If you're cutting a figure out of a magazine, glue it onto stiff paper if it's too limber or floppy.

Be sure that the figure you choose isn't any taller than the width of your card. Illus. 93 shows how to glue your pop-up into place inside the card.

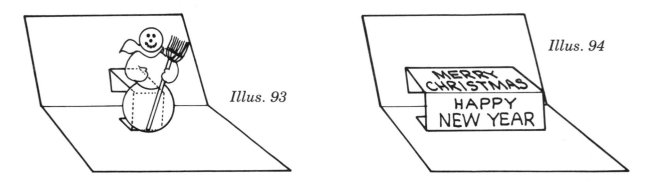

Illus. 93

Illus. 94

When the card closes, the figure is hidden. When the card opens, the figure stands up. Use this idea for a birthday card, an invitation, or any sort of greeting card you like.

If you wish, just write a message on the folded strip. If you do this, make the strip wider than 2″. The drawing in Illus. 94 shows how you can use the folded strip for your message.

You don't have to make all your cards by folding the paper the wide way. Try folding some cards the narrow way so they're tall and thin. Make some fairly small cards for party invitations.

Use your own ideas and experiment with different ways to use these pop-up forms. Your cards will do great things once they're opened.

DOLL CHAINS

People have been folding and cutting paper-doll chains for as long as there's been paper and scissors. This is a folded-paper trick your grandmother certainly knew. Chances are that she and her friends even had little contests to see who could make the chain with the most figures, or to see who could make the fanciest dolls in a chain.

Illus. 95

Your mother may have folded and cut doll chains, as well. Perhaps you've never done this trick with folded paper. If that's the case, let's learn how to do it right now!

For your first doll chain, start with a strip of paper 4″ wide and about 11″ long. Fold this strip of paper into a fan fold (also called an accordion fold). Fold one end of the paper on the dotted line, as shown in Illus. 95. This fold should be about 1¼″ from the end of the paper.

Once this fold has been made, crease the fold and then turn the paper over, with the end still folded. Illus. 96 shows the paper at this point. The dotted line shows the next fold. This fold should come exactly at the edge of the paper you folded over the first time.

When you make this fold, turn the paper over. Make another fold exactly in line with the paper's edge below it. Keep folding and turning until you've folded the entire strip of paper so that it looks like the drawing shown in Illus. 97.

As you fold, be sure that each fold is directly on top of the fold below. If the folds get a bit out of line, the chain of dolls you're going to make won't be ruined, but some of the doll figures may be slightly different from the others.

Illus. 96

Illus. 97

Draw half of the figure you're going to make on the top layer of your folded strip of paper. Begin with a human figure for your first chain.

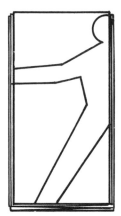

Illus. 98

Illus. 99

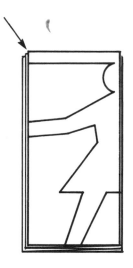

Illus. 100

Before you draw, take a good look at Illus. 98. See how the hand comes right to the fold? Be sure your drawing does this as well. Otherwise, you'll end up with a bunch of single figures, instead of a chain.

As soon as you've drawn half the figure, it's time for some scissor work. Hold the folded paper tightly in one hand while you cut with the other. You don't want the many layers of paper to slip and slide around while you're cutting.

Cut around the figure you just drew, and then unfold the paper. Your reward for a job well done is the chain of dolls shown in Illus. 99. If you end up with half a figure at the end of the chain, just snip it off.

You can make the doll figures taller or shorter, fatter or thinner, just by varying the size of the strip of paper and by making the folds closer together or further apart. What you *don't* want is to have such a thick stack of paper that you can't cut through it.

There's another way to cut out your figures so that the chain is stronger. Illus. 100 shows this method of cutting. Take a look at the strip of paper at the top (an arrow in the drawing points it out).

By leaving this strip of material, your chain is much less likely to pull apart, since you have a solid band

Illus. 101

across the top (just like the one you can see in Illus. 101). If you like this idea, you could leave a strip at the *bottom* of the figures, as well as at the top.

You can join as many strips together as you want, using just a small bit of tape. Be sure you cut each strip of dolls the same size, so you can join several strips together.

You don't have to limit yourself to human figures. Bears, snowmen, and fancy designs are all good ideas. Illus. 102 shows four ideas for doll chains.

Newspaper is a great material for doll chains; the sheets are large and the paper itself is extremely soft and easy to cut. You could use colored paper or gift-wrapping paper and turn your doll chains into party decorations. Think about a string of eggs for Easter, or chains of pumpkins or owls for Halloween.

Remember this folded-paper trick the next time you have to entertain someone (or just yourself) on a rainy day. You can make really fancy chains if you just take a little time.

LOOP-DE-LOOP

One of the best things about learning to do folded-paper tricks is being able to do things others can't. Even better is having the ability to do the seemingly impossible.

Begin the first part of this folded-paper trick by announcing, "I can draw a line on both sides of a piece of

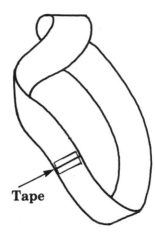

Tape

Illus. 103

paper without lifting the paper off the table *and* without lifting my pencil or pen from the paper."

By now you have everyone's attention. Your audience will tell you that it can't be done. Start by cutting a strip of paper about 2″ wide and as long as the sheet of paper you have handy. Notebook paper is fine, but newspaper works better. A sheet of newspaper is longer than notebook paper, and that helps for this trick.

Hold the strip of paper by both ends. Twist one end half a turn and bring the ends together. Your *Loop De Loop* strip looks like the one shown in Illus. 103. Fasten the two ends together using a strip of tape or glue. Tape's better because your audience may get impatient waiting for the glue to dry.

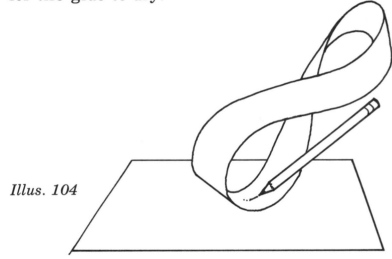

Illus. 104

Now it's time to prove you can do what you claimed. Place the strip on a table or desk top, as shown in Illus. 104. Hold the point of your pen or pencil right on top of the strip, as shown in the drawing.

Now slowly begin to pull on the paper so that it slides along under the point of your pen or pencil. Don't press down too hard, or you'll cut through the paper. Draw a line right down the middle of the strip of paper.

Keep pulling. When you come to the point where the ends are joined, be careful not to tear the joint. Keep on pulling and marking.

After what may seem a long time, you'll be back at the point where you first began your line. Lift your pencil or pen and take a careful look at the strip of paper.

Did you know that this is called a Möbius strip, and that it's named for August F. Möbius, a mathematician?

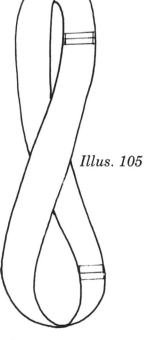

Illus. 105

You'll find that you've drawn a line going all the way around the paper. Not only that, but the line you drew is on both sides of the strip of paper! Stop reading right now and try this trick. It works perfectly.

Once you've shown your audience that you actually drew on both sides of the paper without lifting your pencil or turning the paper over, it's time for the second part of this great trick.

Say, "For the next part of this demonstration, I need to have two narrow strips of paper. I'll just cut this strip in half."

Carefully push the point of your scissors through the strip right along the line you just drew. Put a pad of newspaper on the table and push the scissor point into the strip of paper (while the strip is on the pad of papers). Don't poke your finger or jab the tabletop.

Now cut along the line you just drew. Keep cutting until you're all the way around the strip. Now hold up the results of your work. The strip should look like the one shown in Illus. 105.

As you can see, you don't have two loops of paper. You have one loop that's half as wide and twice as long as the one you first started with. Anyone watching you will now do a quick double take.

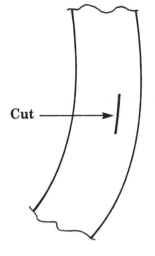

Cut

Illus. 106

Let's move on and do another *Loop-De-Loop* paper trick. This time, cut a strip of paper about 3″ wide. Make a half-twist in this paper, just as you did before, and tape or glue the two loose ends together. Say, "What I really need is a loop about 1″ wide."

Carefully push your scissor point through at a point 1″ from the left side of the paper. The arrow in Illus. 106 shows where to begin cutting.

Keep cutting so that the strip you're cutting off the left side of the paper is 1″ wide. You'll find a strange thing happens as you continue to cut. Eventually, you'll be right back to the point where you started cutting, but at this point you'll be 1″ from the *right* side of the paper.

When you finish cutting, you'll be right where you started. Hold up the loop you cut and you won't have one loop. Instead, you'll have two connected loops. One is twice as large as the other. Try it for yourself, and then find someone to show your newest paper trick.

Don't stop now. Cut another strip of paper about 3″ wide. This strip should be longer than a piece of notebook paper. Use newspaper, or cut two strips of notebook paper and tape them together to make one long strip.

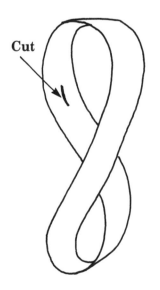

Cut

Illus. 107

Twist one full turn into this strip of paper. As you make the twist, you'll see why you need a longer piece of paper. Don't tear the paper as you make the complete twist. Tape or glue the loose ends together to form a loop. Begin cutting right in the middle of the paper. The arrow in Illus. 107 shows this starting point.

As you cut, keep moving the twisted paper ahead of your scissors. Take your time. Don't ruin the trick by rushing.

When you're back to your starting point, you'll see that now you have *two* connected loops. Now cut each of the two loops in half down the middle, exactly as you did the larger loop. When you finish cutting, you'll have *four* interlocked loops.

Let's do just one more *Loop-De-Loop* paper trick. Begin by cutting a long strip of paper 2″ wide. Once it's cut, put one and one half twists in it. The best way to do this is to hold one end of the paper down on the table with your finger as shown in Illus. 108. Now twist the loose

Illus. 108

end of the paper strip half a turn. Twist it another half turn. Now give it a final half turn and the job is done.

Bring the ends together and tape or glue them together. Next, cut a small strip of paper 1″ wide and about 10″ long. If you have paper that's different from the type you cut for the long strip, use it for the smaller strip. You and your audience can keep a close eye on the small piece.

Form this little strip into a loop around the longer and wider strip you just twisted. Tape together the ends of

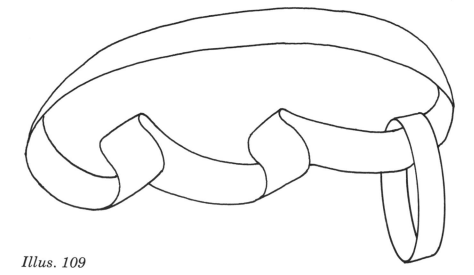

Illus. 109

the small strip and you should have a small loop hooked into a larger one, just like the ones shown in Illus. 109.

Begin cutting the long strip (the one with all those twists in it) down the middle. Take your time and be sure you don't accidentally cut the little loop.

When you finish, you'll have one really big loop with the small loop still hooked into it. There *is* a major surprise ahead—you'll find that the large loop has tied a knot around the little loop.

Show your audience, and ask something like, "Now how did that happen?" Take a bow—you've earned it!

QUICK-CUT STAR

Have you ever noticed how many times you need a star with five perfect points? The next time you're doing a night scene for a bulletin board or for a poster, you'll find that a perfect star will come in handy.

Let's make the first perfect star using a sheet of notebook paper. After you learn the technique, you can use larger or smaller paper depending upon the size you want the finished star to be. Begin by folding the paper in half, so that it looks like the sheet of paper seen in Illus. 110.

Next, locate the middle point of the fold you just made. Do this by bending over (not folding) corner A, shown in Illus. 110, so that it touches corner B.

Once the two corners overlap exactly, pinch the middle to mark it. The arrow in Illus. 111 shows where you're going to pinch the paper together.

Open the paper so that things look like Illus. 112. See where the little pinched fold marks the middle along the bottom of the drawing.

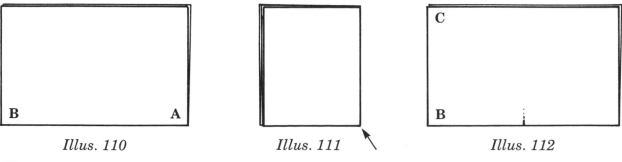

Illus. 110   Illus. 111   Illus. 112

Now locate the middle of the left-hand side of the paper. Do this in the same way that you just found the middle along the bottom. Bend up corner B in Illus. 112 so that it comes up to corner C. Pinch the middle to mark it, and then unfold the paper.

We're now at Illus. 113, with two middle points pinched both on the bottom and on the side. The two arrows point to these middle marks. Fold over the right-hand side of the paper, so that corner A goes right across the middle mark on the left. Illus. 114 shows this step.

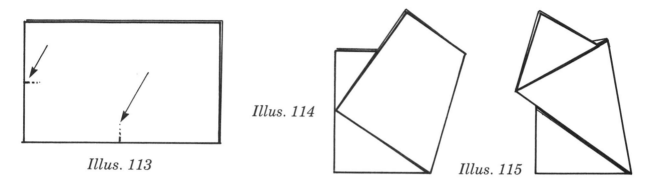

Illus. 113

Illus. 114

Illus. 115

Depending upon the size of your sheet of paper, corner A may extend past that middle mark. If so, great! Be sure that the edge of the paper crosses that pinch mark. However, corner A may not quite reach the edge of the paper. That's fine, too. Just be certain that corner A points right at the pinched middle mark along the side, and everything should come out perfectly.

The next step is easy. Fold over the right side, so that the edge of the paper lies right on top of the pinched point on the side of the paper. Check Illus. 115 to see how things look after making this fold. The edge of the paper should be right on top of corner A, which you folded over in the previous step.

The final fold is no problem. Just fold over corner B on top of the rest of the project, and it should look exactly like Illus. 116. Now a single cut will turn the folded paper into a perfect star with five equal points.

The dotted line shown on Illus. 117 indicates this cut. Make sure that you hold the folded paper firmly so that

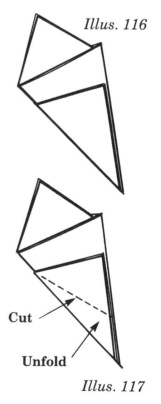

Illus. 116

Cut

Unfold

Illus. 117

the layers don't slip or slide. Make one cut with your scissors.

The arrow in the drawing points to that part of the paper you'll unfold to view your star. The rest of the paper can be discarded.

If you want to have a star with long, fairly narrow points, make a cut like the first one shown in Illus. 118.

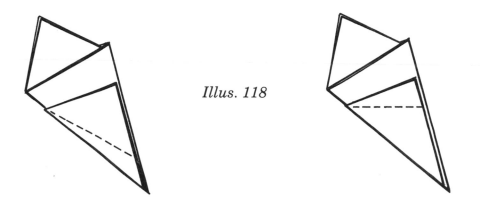

Illus. 118

For a star with shorter, wider points, make a cut at the angle shown in the second drawing in Illus. 118. Check Illus. 119 for the two finished stars.

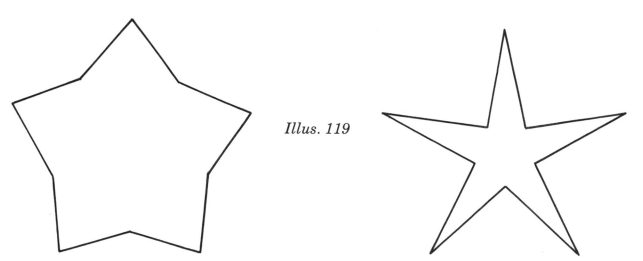

Illus. 119

Practise this on your own, just to be sure that you have the folding and cutting mastered. Now you're ready to become the local star-making expert. You could always use your newly discovered skill to contradict those who will be positive that there's no way to make a star by making just one cut.

NOW YOU SEE IT, NOW YOU DON'T

The folded-paper tricks found in this chapter all have one thing in common: They all involve having things change or disappear right before your eyes. The first pair of projects will amaze others who watch you perform; they won't have any idea how you make the paper do what it does. One thing *is* certain. After you've done these two folded-paper tricks, everyone will want you to demonstrate how to make copies for them.

Two of the tricks in this chapter will turn you into an instant magician with the power to make coins vanish into thin air. The fifth trick is a great little hidden message container; it's so tricky to fold no one will be able to copy it without knowing exactly how you made the original.

MOVING NUMBERS

Your grandparents may very well have played with a flexagon, although your parents probably never did. It's strange but true that many great folded-paper tricks, popular many years ago, were forgotten for many years.

Now's the time to learn how to fold a flexagon. It will perform some great moves to amaze your friends. Your flexagon isn't magic, but it will make some "magic changes" right before your eyes.

You'll need a sheet of notebook paper or typing paper and a bit of tape to put your *Moving Numbers* flexagon together.

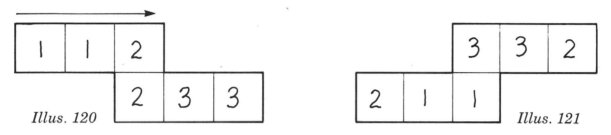

Illus. 120   *Illus. 121*

Draw the figure shown in Illus. 120. Each square should be exactly 2″ × 2″. As soon as you draw the squares, number them as they are in the drawing. Once the squares have been numbered, cut out the flexagon.

Now, turn it over from left to right. The arrow shown in Illus. 120 shows how to turn it correctly. Take hold of the left-hand square with the number 1, and then turn the paper, just as though you were turning a page in a book.

Your flexagon is now in the position shown in Illus. 121. Number the squares exactly as they're numbered in Illus. 121. To check, lift up the square that's indicated by the arrow in the drawing. It should have number 1 on its other side. If it does, you're on the right track.

As soon as you finish numbering the backs of the squares, turn your flexagon over again, so that it looks just like Illus. 120.

Fold the paper along each vertical line between each square. Don't fold the paper along the horizontal line between the two squares containing the 2s. After you've

*Quit clowning around!
We have some serious
folding to do!*

made the four vertical folds, flatten out the paper again. These folds were just to prepare your flexagon for use.

Now it's time to do some serious folding. Fold over the lower right-hand square to the left, so that the 2 on the back shows. Illus. 122 shows this step.

Now fold the upper left-hand squares *under* the project. This puts the two squares containing the 1s on top of the two squares with the 1s facing the back. When this fold is made, the final square (with a 2 on it) will

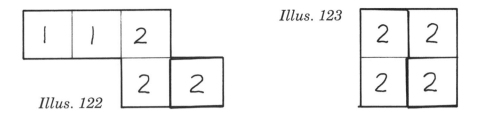

Illus. 123

Illus. 122

appear just as it does in Illus. 123. If your folded-paper trick looks like Illus. 123, everything is perfect.

Before you tape your flexagon together, pick it up *without* letting it unfold. All four squares on the back should have 1s on them.

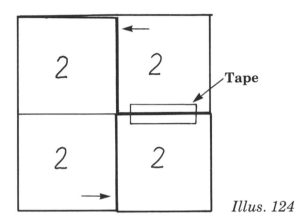

Illus. 124

Use a short strip of tape to fasten the right-hand squares together as shown in Illus. 124. As soon as the tape is in place, your flexagon is ready to perform.

Place your thumbs on the spots shown by the two arrows in the drawing. Gently grasp the edges of those two squares and open the flexagon.

Instead of actually opening, the flexagon will turn itself inside out, right before your eyes. You'll suddenly see four squares, each containing the number 3.

Turn over the flexagon and the 2s are on the back of the folded trick. Hold the flexagon with the 2s facing you, open the flexagon again, and now you're looking at four squares, all containing number 1.

Practise changing numbers often enough so that you know precisely how your flexagon performs. Then you'll be ready to perform this folded-paper trick for others.

If you use colors rather than numbers, choose three colors you like. Instead of writing "1" in four squares, color those squares blue. Instead of "2," color those four squares red. Leave the squares with 3s in them white and you'll have a red, white, and blue flexagon.

If you want to be really special, think of comments to make as you cause the flexagon to change colors right before the eyes of your audience.

A CLOWN, OR NO CLOWN

Now that you know how flexagons work, let's make a more complicated folded-paper puzzle. This puzzle is *really* astounding.

Once again, use a sheet of notebook paper or typing paper. Draw the twelve squares, as shown in Illus. 125. Each square must be *exactly* 2" × 2".

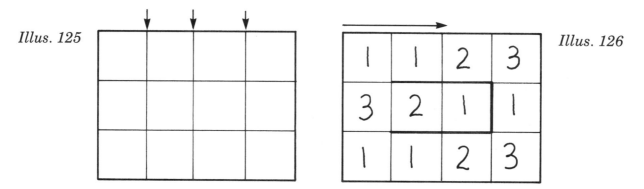

Illus. 125

Illus. 126

Now cut away any excess paper on the sheet. Once you've drawn the twelve squares, fold the project along the three vertical lines indicated by the arrows in Illus. 125. Once the folds are in place, unfold the paper again. Number the squares just as they're shown in Illus. 126.

As soon as you've finished numbering, do some very careful scissor work. The dark cut lines around the middle pair of squares should be cut now. Don't start cutting until you check the drawing carefully. Be sure that you make the three cuts *exactly* as they're shown in Illus. 126.

When you push the point of your scissors through the paper, be careful not to poke yourself. Put a pad of newspaper under the paper and use the newspaper as backing

By any chance have you seen the rest of the newspaper?

to protect both your fingers and the table, as you push the scissors through the paper.

As soon as you've made the necessary cuts, turn the paper over, from left to right. The arrow in Illus. 126 shows the direction to turn the paper. It's just like turning the page in a book.

Number the six squares with 2s and 3s, as shown in Illus. 127. Draw the clown's head at the upper left. Check the drawing to see how the hat and the head are centered along the fold line between the two squares. This alignment is necessary, because you want your clown's body to line up correctly once you perform this trick.

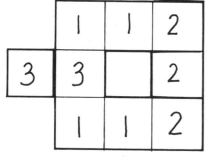

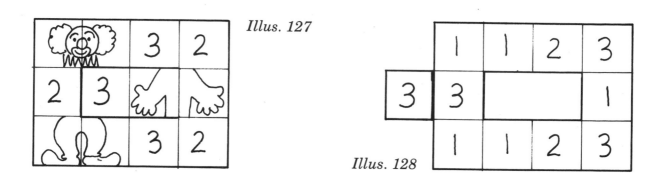

Next, draw the neck and the body of the clown in the two right-hand squares in the middle row. Just as you did before, center the neck and the body on the fold.

Draw a pair of legs for the clown in the two squares at the lower left. The legs should be centered on the fold, and they should be just as wide as the lower part of the clown's torso. That's so your clown doesn't look out of line once you line it up in a few minutes.

Turn the paper over so that it looks like Illus. 126.

Fold the center squares under and to the left. When you finish this fold, your flexagon should look just like the one shown in Illus. 128.

Your next fold brings you to Illus. 129. Fold the right-hand column of squares under the rest of the paper. This brings a "2" into view in the open space in the middle of the column, as shown in Illus. 129.

Now bring over the square that's sticking out at the left, so that it's now folded over the *front* of the flexagon. As you can see in Illus. 130, this step gives you an entire column of 1s at the left of the flexagon.

Make the final fold by folding back the right-hand column *under* the rest of the flexagon. Once this fold is

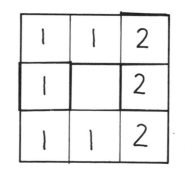

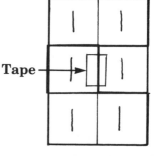

Illus. 129 *Illus. 130* *Illus. 131*

made, your flexagon should look like Illus. 131. You're looking at six squares—all of them contain 1s.

Hold the flexagon so that it doesn't unfold and then check the back. You should see all six squares with 2s in them.

Now apply a bit of tape. The tape is shown in Illus. 131. This step is very important and must be done correctly. Make absolutely certain that the tape touches only the two squares containing 1s (as shown in the drawing). Don't let the tape fasten onto the paper beneath the left-hand square (the square you folded over the top in Illus. 130).

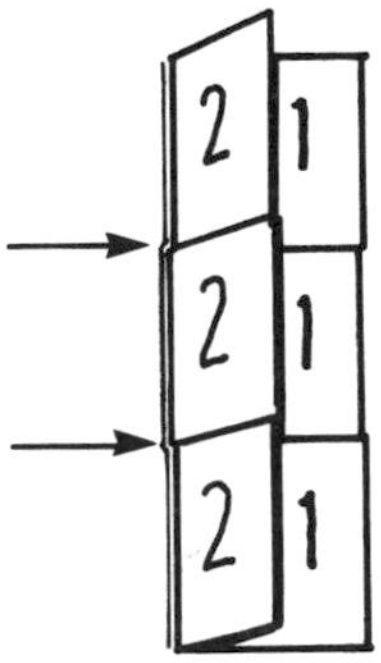

Making your flexagon perform takes just a bit of practice. Don't get discouraged if it doesn't do exactly what it should the first time you try it. This folded-paper trick will take just a few minutes to perform correctly.

Fold over the left column of the flexagon, so that it looks like Illus. 132.

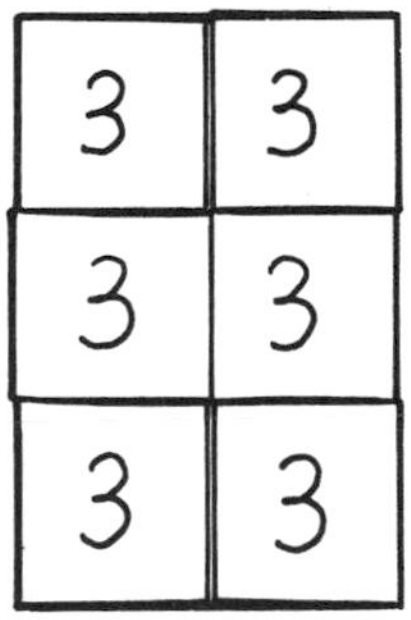

Grasp it at the points shown by the two arrows and open it up to your right. Every square in front of you has a 3 in it, as shown in Illus. 133.

Let's find the clown hidden inside the folded paper. Fold back both sides so that your flexagon looks like the one shown in Illus. 134. Just fold the sides partway back.

Place your thumbs at the points shown by the arrows in Illus. 134. Pull your thumbs apart just a bit and continue folding the sides of the project back towards each other.

Illus. 132

Illus. 133

Illus. 134

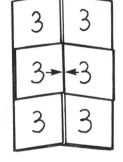

Illus. 135

Now the clown will appear, as shown in Illus. 135. If you check the back of the flexagon, you'll see that all the squares have the number "3".

To make the clown vanish, fold the sides towards you, so that the clown is in the middle of the fold. Pull apart the back edges, and you'll be looking at 3s again.

Fold the 3s together and open the sides from the back, and six 2s will stare you in the face. Turn the paper over and there are all those 1s.

Practise this flexagon and experiment with it. Work out your own series of folds and openings so that you always know exactly how each move will change the flexagon. Once you're confident you know exactly how to make the clown come and go, it's time to perform your latest and greatest folded-paper trick.

VANISHING COIN

This folded-paper trick is fun to make and master, and then it's even more fun to perform as a magic trick. It will leave others wondering whether or not to believe their eyes.

Begin with two pieces of very stiff material, each 3″ × 6″. File folders are great for this project because both sides are identical. Don't use cereal-box material—you will see why when you finish the trick.

Lay the pieces side by side, as shown in Illus. 136. Now cut two pieces of the same material, each 2″ square. Tape them onto the two larger pieces, so that things look like Illus. 137. As you tape each 2″ square into place, make sure that there's enough space between it and the larger section so that you'll be able to slip a coin into this little holder. You can bend up the little squares just a bit in the middle before you tape them down into place to provide the space you need.

When you're taping, be sure that the two sections look exactly alike.

Now cut four strips of paper, each ¾″ wide and 7″ long. Place the strips of paper on top of and beneath the two sections of material, so that they look like the project pictured in Illus. 138. The dotted lines in the illustration show where the paper strips run under the sections of stiff file-folder material.

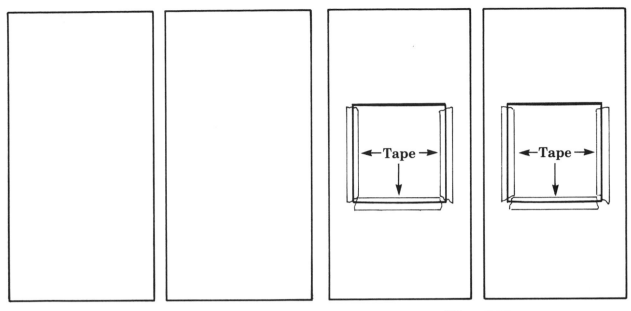

Illus. 136   *Illus. 137*

Fold both ends of paper strip over the edges of the sections of stiff file-folder material. Be sure to leave about ⅛″ of space between the two sections. Illus. 139 shows the ends bent into place, and it also shows the space between the two sections. As you can see, the ends of the two middle strips are now folded under at the left and taped or glued on the bottom side of the material.

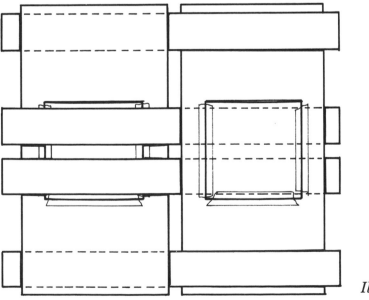

Illus. 138

What a mess! Didn't you try that out first?

The same is true of the ends of the top and bottom strips on the right-hand section of stiff file-folder material.

Now it's magic time! Practise this trick by yourself often enough to be certain that you know what to expect before you start performing in public.

Fold the left-hand side *under*, so that all you can see is the right-hand side. Illus. 140 shows this step. This is how you'll present your folded-paper trick when you perform in public.

Slip a coin into the little square. Now fold this section over to the left. Keep on folding until the two sides are pressed together. Your trick should look like Illus. 141. The two squares of stiff material (the coin holders) face each other inside the folded trick.

Open the two sections of the trick. Lift up on the left-hand side of the top layer. The arrow in Illus. 141 shows where to lift.

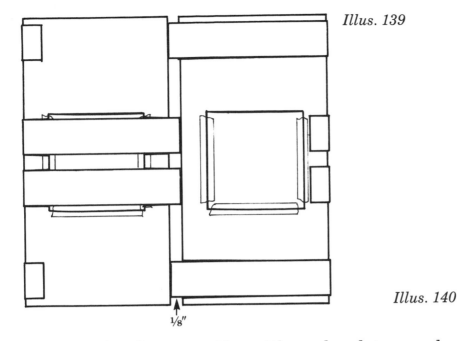

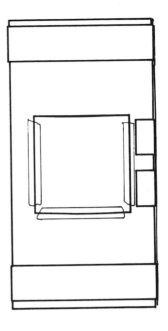

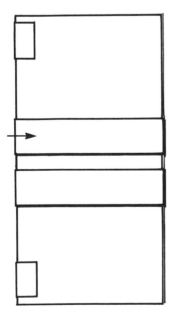

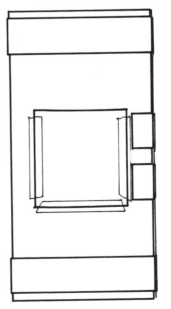

Illus. 139

Illus. 140

⅛″

As you raise the top section with one hand, turn under the bottom section using your other hand. When you finish this move, you've reached Illus. 142.

Be sure you're holding the coin pocket (on the underneath side) closed with a finger. Tip the trick forward, so that someone in your audience can pull up on the open side of the coin holder on top of the folder. The coin is gone. You've just done a super folded-paper magic trick.

Illus. 141

Illus. 142

Repeat the same steps, and suddenly there will be a coin inside the coin holder on top of the trick.

Practise this until you're positive you know how to make the folds without letting anyone see that there are two coin holders. You'll find that you'll need to turn the folder a bit so that the top shields the bottom as you're opening and closing the folder.

This folded-paper trick is sure to impress your audience. Don't ever let anyone get hold of the folder! Be sure you hold the folder so that no one can look at it from underneath.

FOR SECRET MESSAGES ONLY

One of the great things about sending a message is keeping it secret.

This message holder is *certain* to keep its contents a secret. In fact, it's so secret that unless you actually *show* someone how to fold the message holder, no one will ever be able to reproduce it exactly.

First turn a sheet of notebook paper or typing paper into a square. Keep the leftover strip of paper to write your first secret message on.

When you folded the rectangle of paper to turn it into a square, you used one diagonal fold. It's shown in Illus. 143. The dotted line in the drawing indicates your next fold—the other diagonal.

Illus. 143

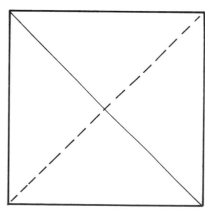

Illus. 144

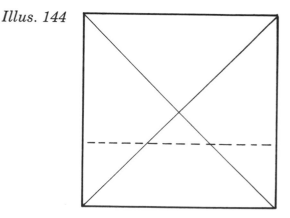

With both diagonal folds in place, things should look like Illus. 144. The dotted line in Illus. 144 shows your

82

next fold. This fold should be exactly one-third of the way up from the bottom of the page.

If you've got a good eye, go ahead and make the fold. If you're not certain that you can estimate one-third the distance, use a ruler. Notebook paper and typing paper are both usually 8½″ wide, and your square is 8½″ square. Measure up from the bottom of the page just a bit more than 2¾″. If you're using paper of a different size, measure it and divide by three to see where to make this fold.

Try to be exact, but don't worry if your fold is off by just a bit. Your project won't be ruined.

Crease this fold, then unfold it. Illus. 145 shows the paper with this fold in place; it also shows a dotted line for your next fold.

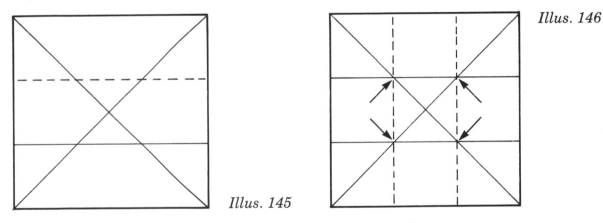

Illus. 146

Illus. 145

To make the next fold, bring the top of the paper down to the fold you just made, and then crease the new fold. Once again, unfold the paper.

Illus. 146 shows these folds in place. The two dotted lines show your next pair of folds. These folds are easy, since you already have some guide folds in place. Check the arrows in the drawing.

Fold each side of the paper so that the fold runs through the point where two other folds intersect. The arrows show these points.

Crease both folds and unfold the paper once more. Illus. 147 shows how things look with all these folds in place. Now fold over the right-hand edge of the project, so that it looks like Illus. 148. Now fold up the bottom edge, and your mailer is seen in Illus. 149.

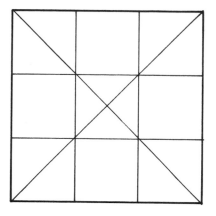

Illus. 147

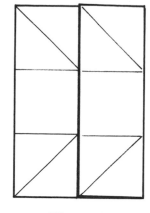

Illus. 148

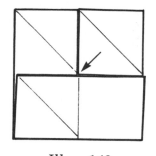

Illus. 149

Here comes the fun! Take hold of the corner of the paper at the point shown by the arrow in Illus. 149. Turn that corner inside out. Now you're reversing a couple of the folds you made earlier.

Check Illus. 150 to see what the paper will look like once you turn that corner inside out. Make certain that you don't have any wrinkles, and that your reversed folds follow the original fold lines. When everything looks like Illus. 150, crease the folds into place.

Once you've creased these folds, unfold the paper. Turn the paper a quarter turn. The arrow in Illus. 150 shows the direction of this turn. Now fold the right side *over* and the bottom edge *up*, just as you did before. Just repeat the steps shown in Illus. 148 and Illus. 149. Then, pull the corner out by reversing the folds, so that this next corner looks like the one shown in Illus. 150.

Crease the folds, unfold the paper, give it a quarter turn, and repeat the process. Then, do the entire performance one more time, so that you've turned all four corners inside out.

As soon as you've done all that folding and creasing, move on to the next step. Go back and pull out each corner into a point like the one you formed in Illus. 150. This time leave the points out. When all four corners have been pulled back out into points, your mailer should look exactly like Illus. 151.

Don't rush with this step. Take your time and work with one point at a time. The first three are easy. They should just pop right into place. The fourth point may

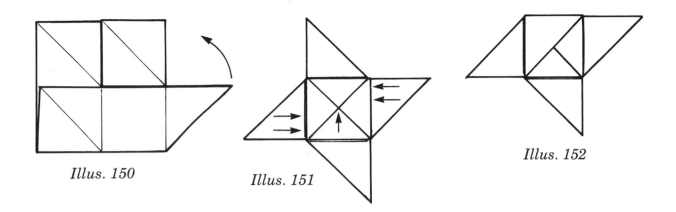

Illus. 150

Illus. 151

Illus. 152

look as though it's hidden, but it's there. Work slowly, don't panic, and pull out the fourth and final point into place.

Now's the time to slip your message into the mailer. The arrow points to a tiny opening in Illus. 151. You don't have to roll your message into a tiny ball or cylinder and push it through that little opening. Write your message on a small sheet of paper, fold the sheet so that it's about 1″ square.

Take hold of the mailer on the two sides indicated by the double arrows shown in Illus. 151. Pull those sides apart just a bit and slip the message inside. Once the note is safely inside the mailer, let the sides come back together and finish the last few folds. You're almost home now. The tricky part is behind you.

Fold the top point down and your mailer should look like Illus. 152. Fold over the point at the left and you've reached the step shown in Illus. 153. When you fold up the bottom point, you've reached Illus. 154. The arrow in the drawing shows where you'll tuck under the right-hand point when you fold it into place.

Once the last point is folded over and tucked in, your mailer should look like Illus. 155.

Although this first mailer took several minutes to make, your next one can be folded quite quickly. You'll pick up speed with each mailer you fold.

Message mailers can be any size. Start with a square piece of material. By using gift-wrapping paper, you can

Illus. 153

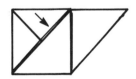

Illus. 154

Illus. 155

use this folded-paper trick to make envelopes for greeting cards. You could even use it to wrap flat presents, such as small books.

As for sending secret messages, just remember that your teacher may not think that it's important to fold mailers in class. Keep that in mind and you may save yourself some trouble.

Is this supposed to be me?

WHERE'D THE COIN GO?

Let's learn to do one more fine magic trick with folded paper.

For this folded-paper trick you'll use five squares of paper. Make one 8½″ square. You're probably using notebook paper or typing paper, so this is a perfect-size square to make.

You'll have to use a ruler for the next squares. You need two squares—6″ or 6½″ on a side. You'll also be using two squares 4″ or 4½″ on each side. You can cut one 6″ square and one 4″ square from a single sheet of notebook paper.

Once the five squares of paper are ready, it's folding time. Let's start with the large square. Fold up the bottom edge along the dotted line, as shown in Illus. 156. This fold should be 2½″ from the bottom edge. That's just slightly less than one-third the distance from the top to the bottom of the square.

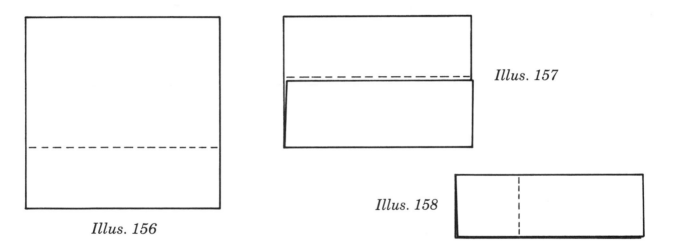

Illus. 157

Illus. 158

Illus. 156

When that fold is in place, the paper should look like Illus. 157. The dotted line in Illus. 157 shows the next fold.

To make the second fold, bring down the top edge so that it comes exactly to the bottom edge. Now your project should look like the one shown in Illus. 158.

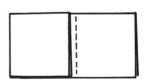

Illus. 159

The dotted line shown in Illus. 158 is your next fold; it's about 2¾″ in from the left side. Once you've made this fold, you've reached Illus. 159.

Fold over the right-hand side on the dotted line shown in the drawing. Bring the right-hand edge of the paper right over to the fold, and your square should be folded neatly into the little packet seen in Illus. 160.

Illus. 160

Now let's deal with the 6″ squares. Fold both of them exactly as you just folded the 8½″ square. You'll repeat the five steps shown in Illus. 156 to Illus. 160 for each square, but the folds will differ in size. Fold up the bottom edge about 1¾″. Fold down the top edge so that it meets the bottom fold. Fold over the left side 2″. Bring over the right side so that the edge reaches the fold. The job's done!

Fold the second 6″ square exactly as you did the first one. This is very important. The folds must be in the exact same location for both of these squares of paper, since the section in the middle of one paper must be precisely the same size as the middle section of the other paper.

Once these two squares are folded (so they look like Illus. 160) you'll need to do a bit of gluing. Hold the two folded squares back to back. Spread glue on the back (actually the middle section, once the square is unfolded) of one paper and glue the two sheets together.

Set these squares aside as the glue dries. Now fold the small squares. Once again, you'll follow the same procedure you've used for the other paper squares. Fold up the bottom ½″ or ¾″. Fold down the top edge to the bottom fold. Fold over the left side 1¼″. Fold over the right side, and you've got another little packet. It should look like Illus. 160.

Repeat the process for the other small square. Make sure its folds are the same size as the ones in the first small square.

After all this folding, let's see how this folded-paper trick works.

Leave the smallest squares folded. Unfold both parts of the medium squares—they're glued together at the middle.

Place one small square in the middle of the medium square (as shown in Illus. 161). Make sure that the back of the small square (that's its middle section) faces you.

Refold the medium-sized square so that the small square is hidden inside. When you refold, fold in the same order that you originally folded the paper. That's bottom, top, left side, and right side.

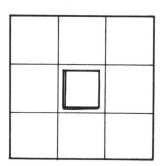

Illus. 161

Turn over the medium-sized square and place the other small square inside. Fold the medium-sized square over the small one, just as you did for the other side.

Unfold the largest square, slip the packet of all the other squares inside, and refold the big square. Now you're ready for the trick!

Unfold the big square, but don't remove the packet inside. Now things should look like Illus. 162. Open the middle square, and now we're at Illus. 163.

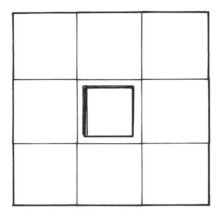
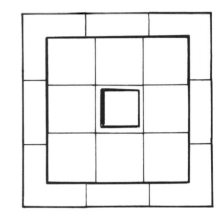

Illus. 162   *Illus. 163*

Your audience has no way of knowing that there's another set of squares glued onto the back of the middle-sized square. All that's visible is the little square inside, and it's still folded.

Open up the small square and your folded paper trick should look like Illus. 164. Place a coin in the middle of the unfolded small square. Refold this small square, just as you've been folding squares for some time now. That's bottom, top, left side, and right side. You'll always follow

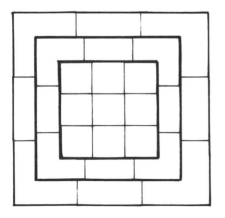
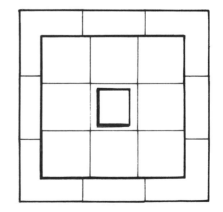

Illus. 164   *Illus. 165*

this same pattern because that's the way the folds fit together.

Turn over the paper with the coin inside, so that the back of the paper faces you. Now you're at Illus. 165.

Refold the middle square around the small one. Turn over the middle square so that its back or middle section faces you. Illus. 166 shows the trick at this point.

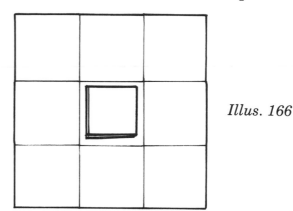

Illus. 166

Illus. 167

The next step is to fold up the final square to enclose the rest of the papers. Illus. 167 shows it all folded in place.

If you want to make this look really magical, say some magic words, wave your hands over the papers, or anything else to impress your audience.

After working your magic, turn over the packet and it's time to start unfolding. Open the large square. Don't turn over the middle square, just unfold it.

Turn over the small square, open it, and to everyone's surprise (except yours) the coin has vanished!

To make the coin reappear, fold the small section and turn it over. Refold the middle section and turn it over. Now fold the large square around the others. Do your magic moves again, and it's time to unfold one more time.

Unfold the large square. Open up the middle square without turning it over. Now undo the small square and there, magically, is the coin!

Practise this trick a few times just to be sure you know when to turn over the folded squares. Once you've perfected the moves, find an audience and prepare to mystify them!

JUST A SIMPLE FOLD OR TWO

It's great fun to surprise people with a trick they aren't expecting. It's especially fun to do the seemingly impossible. Show others that something that *sounds* simple is either extremely difficult, or actually impossible!

The tricks in this chapter are very simple to set up. Some require only one fold to get things going. Several of these tricks have unexpected results to grab people's attention. A couple of the tricks are real shockers, when something *sounding* quite simple turns out to be completely impossible. All of the tricks are easy to do and they're certain to surprise your audience.

WHAT KEEPS IT THERE?

This first trick is so easy *anyone* can do it. But, this quick trick will also leave many people puzzled.

Cut a piece of notebook paper 3″ wide by 6″ long. Make the fold shown by the dotted line in Illus. 168.

When you perform this trick for others, make a fuss about getting the fold exactly right. Tell your audience that if you mess up the fold, the trick won't work, and that you'll have to start all over again.

The fold really has nothing to do with how the trick works. Just fold up about ½″ of the paper's end. The trick works perfectly with a flat sheet of paper, but by folding the paper, you distract your audience's attention from what's really happening.

Illus. 168

Hold the paper in your hand so that the folded end faces up. This is important. If you hold the fold *down*, the trick may well be on *you* when this simple little puzzler doesn't work.

Now comes the magic that makes the trick work. Scuff your feet across the carpet as you walk towards a wall, a door, or the end of a bookcase or a cupboard, Don't be obvious about scuffing your feet, or you'll give the trick away. Just shuffle along.

Shuffle your feet to pick up a charge of static electricity from the carpet. You *must* perform this trick on a carpeted floor.

When you reach the door, cabinet, wall, or whatever, mumble some magical words and use the palm of your hand to press the paper against the flat surface of the wall, door, etc. Remove your hand, and the paper will remain stuck to the wall.

Pull the paper off the surface, and then replace it. The paper will probably stick again. Depending upon how much static electricity you built up as you scuffed across the floor, the paper may be removed and replaced several times.

Eventually, the paper will *not* stick to the surface. When that happens, announce that your magic fold has lost its power. Refold the paper along the dotted line, as shown in Illus. 169.

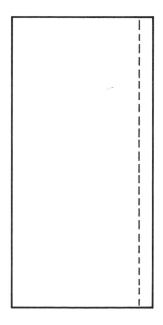

Illus. 169

Once again, the refolding just draws attention away from what's *really* keeping the paper on the wall.

Repeat the shuffle, and press the paper to the wall. When it sticks in place, announce that *fortunately* you've made another magic fold in just the right place.

Make different folds to keep this trick going. Young children and even an older audience won't catch on if you conceal your foot-scuffing routine.

This trick works best in dry weather. Rehearse it before you perform it. On a damp day you might not be able to build up the static charge you need. Almost always you'll be able to generate enough static electricity to make this simple trick work like a charm.

HERE'S A SPECIAL MESSAGE, JUST FOR YOU

Two quick folds and two sentences will turn a sheet of paper into a message. Your victims will read it several times before they realize that you've tricked them.

Cut a sheet of paper so that it's about 3″ wide by 8″ long. Make the two folds indicated by the dotted lines shown in Illus. 170. Each fold should be 2″ from either end of the paper.

Once you've made the folds, unfold the paper and refold the ends backwards, instead of forward. This will make it easy for you to fold the ends, either to the front or to the back.

Now print (in large letters) the sentence (shown in Illus. 171) on the front of the paper, between the folds.

Turn the paper over and print the message (seen in Illus. 172) on the back. Keep the sentence between the fold lines.

Here's how to present this folded-paper trick. Fold both ends over the message that reads READ THE OTHER SIDE TO LEARN HOW TO FOOL PEOPLE. Tell your victim you have something for him to read.

Lift the flaps so that he can read the message. When you lift the flaps, fold them back and under to cover the message on the *back* of the paper.

Illus. 170

Illus. 171

As soon as your victim reads the first message, turn over the paper and open the flaps so that the second message appears. Say that some people are harder to fool than others.

Let your victim turn the paper over to reread the front if he wishes. Don't laugh aloud if this happens.

Don't be surprised when some people turn the paper over and over several times before they realize how easily they've just been fooled.

Turn the paper over to find out how easy people are to fool

Illus. 172

Are you trying to make a fool out of me?

NO TOUCHING!

This folded-paper trick will prove that you're sharper than anyone ever suspected.

Begin with a page from a newspaper. It really doesn't matter whether it's from a large or a small newspaper. What's important is the way you present this trick to others.

Say that you've been doing a lot of research with folding paper, and that you've made a fantastic discovery. "In fact, I've found how to fold this sheet of newspaper in such a way that two people can stand on it and still not be able to touch the top of each other's heads at the same time."

Someone in the audience will surely ask whether the two people will be facing each other.

Smile and say, "Yes, the two people will face one another." When you first announce your trick, you could tell the audience that the two people will face each other. It's up to you.

Probably someone will ask, "Is one standing and the other kneeling?"

Reply, "That's entirely up to them," or some such answer.

Before the audience can ask any more questions, make a big fuss while folding the paper. Fold it, unfold it, crease a fold, do whatever you wish. Fold down a couple of corners for effect. How you fold it doesn't matter at all. What matters is that you end up with a sheet of paper that's as long as it was to start with and just wide enough for a person to stand with both feet on either end.

Once you've entertained your audience with all the folding, and you have their curiosity aroused, it's time to prove that you can perform this trick. You could select two victims to demonstrate how right you are. If you wish, *you* could stand on one end of the paper and a member of the audience on the other.

Have one person stand in a doorway, just inside the door. Place the paper on the floor (as shown in Illus. 173) so that it extends past the doorway on both sides of the door.

Close the door; someone should be standing on one end of the paper on the *other* side of the door. At this point everyone should realize just how clever you really are.

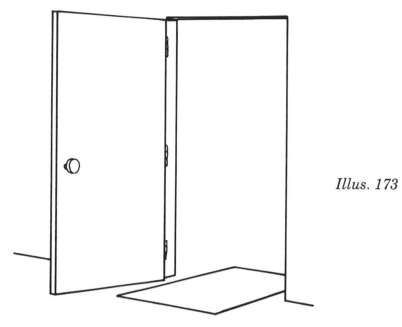

Illus. 173

It's easy for two people to stand on both ends of the paper with the closed door between them. It's also impossible for them to touch the top of each other's head at the same time.

If there's lots of space beneath the door, someone may try to bend over, so that his head touches the floor, and he'll then ask the other to reach under the door.

This is all well and good, but it's impossible to get into that position with both feet still planted firmly on the end of the paper. Besides, you said it would be impossible for both to touch the top of each other's head at the same time. Once again, you're exactly right.

ANYONE CAN FOLD PAPER

Once you become known as an expert folded-paper trickster, you'll be surprised how often someone will ask you to do another trick. People enjoy seeing how tricks work, and most people don't mind being tricked. They're more than willing to go out and play the same trick on someone else!

This folded-paper trick sounds simple, but it's truly impossible. Once you (casually) remark that it's impossible, there will always be someone wanting to prove you wrong.

Hold up a sheet of notebook paper. Fold it once in the middle and leave it folded, so that it looks like Illus. 174.

Illus. 174

Pretend to study it. Make sure you have everyone's attention. Say, "I'll bet it's impossible to fold this paper in half six more times. No," shaking your head, "Maybe seven more times. That would only be if a person were *really* strong."

Someone will accept your challenge. After all, anyone can fold paper in half. Make your next fold either the

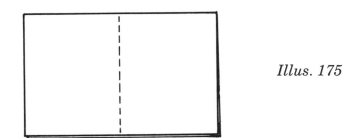   *Illus. 175*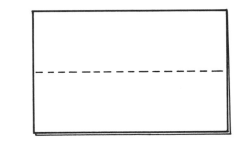

long way or the short way; fold the paper exactly in half. Illus. 175 shows both alternative folds.

The rules of this trick state that each new fold must be in the middle of the paper and that the paper *must* remain folded after each new fold.

Now that you've folded and folded and folded that sheet of notebook paper, you have a good idea what will happen.

When someone from your audience fails to make the eighth fold in the sheet of notebook paper, one thing will certainly happen. Someone will ask for a larger sheet of paper.

A double sheet of newspaper is perfect. Since the sheet is so large, tell your eager paper folder to go for ten folds. He or she will fail. Try it for yourself, just to be sure.

Even if you use a large sheet of thin tissue paper or thin wrapping paper, no one can fold the paper in half ten times and have the folds stay in place. It just can't be done.

Make the challenge fit the person. Let human nature do the rest. Few people can resist the urge to prove that you don't know what you're talking about, especially when you tell them that something is impossible.

FOLDING'S EASY, COUNTING'S HARD

It takes about twenty seconds to fold the paper for this

Don't try this if your paper's too thick to cut!

trick. Then, depending upon skill, luck, and determination, it can take fifteen minutes or more to do a simple counting job.

Make a square from a sheet of notebook paper or similar paper. Fold the square in half. Unfold the square so that it looks like Illus. 176.

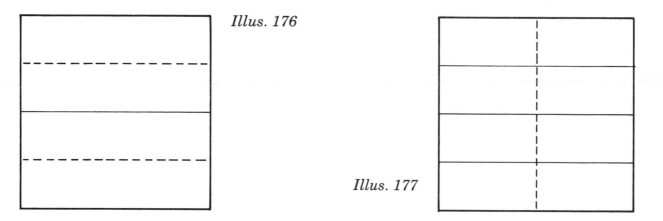

Illus. 176

Illus. 177

Fold the top edge along the dotted line as shown in Illus. 176 so that the edge comes right to the middle fold. Do the same with the bottom edge.

Once the two folds are made and creased, unfold the paper. The fold lines are shown in Illus. 177.

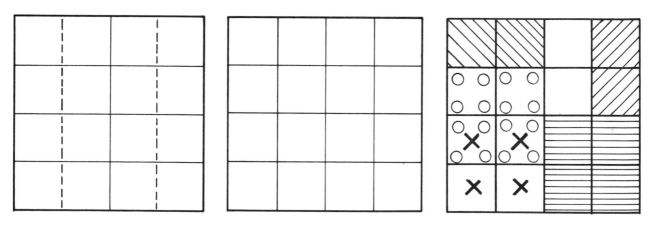

Illus. 178   *Illus. 179*   *Illus. 180*

Now fold the paper in half along the dotted line, as shown in Illus. 177. Once the fold has been made, unfold it and it should look like Illus. 178. The dotted lines in Illus. 178 indicate your next pair of folds.

Fold in both sides so that their edges meet at the middle fold. Crease the folds. Unfold the paper and flatten it out so that it looks like Illus. 179.

Your folding is done! Now let's see how well you count. Once you've perfected your counting skills, use this folded-paper trick to puzzle and perplex your friends.

Count all the rectangles you've created on the square sheet of paper. Remember that a rectangle is any two-dimensional figure with four straight sides and four square corners. A square is also a rectangle.

It's easy to count the small rectangles you created by making the six folds. Now the job gets a bit more difficult.

Two folded rectangles side by side combine to make one larger rectangle. The upper left-hand corner shown in Illus. 180 shows one of these rectangles. The upper right-hand corner of Illus. 180 shows another way to look at a pair of rectangles joined to form a larger one.

Combine four small rectangles and you'll have one even larger one, as shown in the lower left-hand corner of Illus. 180.

Now that you know what to look for, consider one more thing. It's possible for the rectangles to overlap one another. In other words, the four small rectangles (with

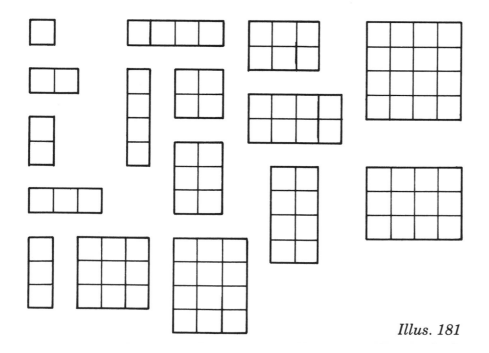

Illus. 181

the little circles in them) obviously form a larger rectangle. Look at the four small rectangles containing Xs. They also form a larger rectangle overlapping the rectangle with the little circles.

Keep track of your rectangle count by first counting the rectangles of the same size, until you're positive you've counted all of them. Record that number and move on to all the rectangles of another size. It helps to make a sketch of the various rectangular shapes and note the number you locate beside the sketch. Illus. 181 will help you visualize some of the various rectangles you're looking for.

Once you've mastered this tricky bit of counting, search for those who think they're experts at dealing with folded paper.

There are *100* rectangles on your folded paper. Don't give up until you find *all* of them.

RIGHT CAN'T BE WRONG

This nifty little trick is so simple that you can learn it in a minute. It's tricky enough so that others won't figure it out. You'll be able to perform it again and again.

Fold a sheet of paper in half and then unfold it. Use a full sheet of notebook paper if you wish, but a smaller sheet is easier to handle. Try a sheet of paper about 4″ by 6″ and see how it works. If you're performing in front of large groups, a large, full sheet of paper is better because you can make large letters on it.

After you've unfolded the paper, write the word RIGHT in capital letters above the fold, so it looks like Illus. 182.

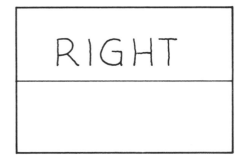

Illus. 182

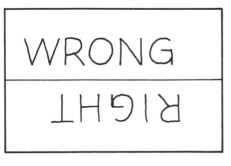

Illus. 183

Turn the paper around and print WRONG in capital letters, as shown in Illus. 183. Now make this folded-paper trick work for you! Turn the paper so RIGHT is on top. This leaves WRONG upside-down.

Illus. 184

Illus. 185

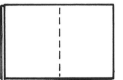

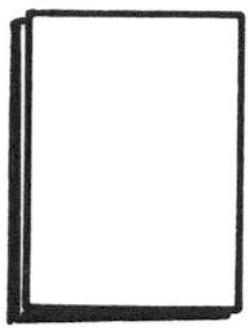

Illus. 186

Fold down the top of the paper along the original fold. Illus. 184 shows the fold in place. The dotted line in Illus. 184 shows your next fold.

Fold over the right side to the left and you've reached Illus. 185. The dotted line indicates your next fold.

Again, fold the right side over to the left. Now you're at Illus. 186.

Next, unfold the back from left to right to arrive at Illus. 187. Here's the important step. Unfold the back of the paper from right to left! Now you're at Illus. 188.

Unfold the top just by lifting up. What you see now is shown in Illus. 189.

Once you've shown that you can turn RIGHT into WRONG, make this trick a bit more interesting by going through the folding and unfolding and having RIGHT come up in-

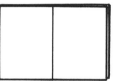

Illus. 187

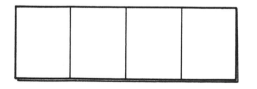

Illus. 188

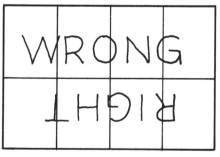

Illus. 189

stead of WRONG. All you have to do is change the way you unfold the paper.

First unfold the back from left to right—this brings you to Illus. 187. Now, instead of unfolding the back as you did before, unfold the front from right to left. Open the top by lifting it up, and now you'll be looking at RIGHT, rather than WRONG.

Take a minute or two, follow the directions, and learn how to change RIGHT to WRONG, or how to leave RIGHT just as it is. Once you have WRONG upright you can change it back to RIGHT, just as you changed RIGHT to WRONG. If this sounds confusing, it really isn't. Just practise it a time or two, and you'll get the hang of it.

As soon as you're sure of your moves, you'll be able to change RIGHT to WRONG and back again with the words facing an audience.

Hold the paper in front of you with the words facing away from you. Fold over the top, fold it in half, and then in half again. The folds in the paper go in the proper direction and will guide you.

When you unfold, unfold the paper halfway, and then decide whether you want to change the word or keep it the same. To change the word, unfold from the back. To keep the word the same, unfold from the front. It's simple once you practise it once or twice.

Instead of using the words RIGHT or WRONG, substitute other words, or even people's names. Color half the paper one color, and color the other half another color.

Remember to keep your folding and unfolding going without any breaks. It will take a long time for others to realize what you're doing. Some people *never* figure out this great folded-paper trick.

STRONGER THAN YOU'D THINK

This folded-paper trick demonstrates your paper-folding skills, or it can be used to trick others.

If you want people to challenge your ability, place two glasses (the same size) upside down in front of you. If you don't have two glasses handy, two books or two soup cans will work as well. Whatever you use, both items should be the same height.

Place a file card or a piece of cereal-box material on top of both glasses, as shown in Illus. 190.

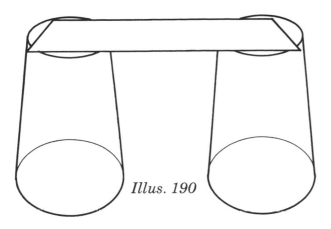

Illus. 190

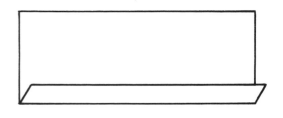

Illus. 191

Press down on the middle of the file card (or other material) and it will bow in the middle. Say, "I'll bet this file card is strong enough to hold a can of soup between these two glasses."

Your audience can see that the card is bending as you lightly push down on it. It can't support a can of soup, or any item of that weight.

Now it's time to perform your trick! Remove the file card and begin making a fan fold. Illus. 191 shows the first fold.

This fold should be anywhere from ⅜″ to ½″ wide. Continue folding the card into a fan (or accordion) by folding it back and forth until you reach the point shown in Illus. 192. Crease each fold *well* so all the folds stay in place. Now set the folded file card back on top of the glasses. Your setup now looks like Illus. 193.

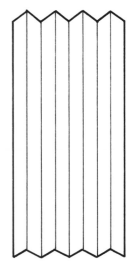

Illus. 192

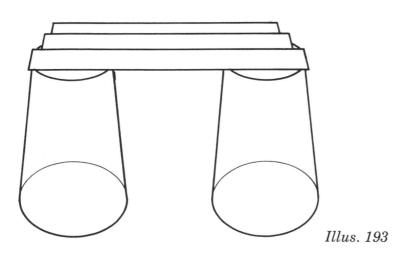

Illus. 193

Make sure that the folds in the fan stay fairly close together. Carefully set a can of soup or some other weight on the card. The folded card will hold it easily.

Now that you see how this works, experiment with a sheet (or part of a sheet) of notebook paper. You will be amazed how much weight it can support once it's folded into a proper fan.

FOLD AND PERFORM

You'll enjoy folding the tricks in this chapter on your own. You'll have lots more fun when you perform your newly learned trick for others.

Folded-paper tricks are like many things in life. They're great when you do them on your own, but they're even better when you share them with others.

PERFECT BALANCE

You can balance a sheet of notebook paper on the tip of your finger, if you know how. All that's necessary is to make one fold in the paper, and you'll be ready to do your balancing act.

This trick works with just about any sheet of paper. Begin with a sheet of notebook paper or typing paper. Later, after you've seen how this folded-paper trick works, try it using a larger sheet of paper (such as the side of a large grocery bag) or even using a sheet of newspaper.

Try this balancing act the first time using a sheet of paper that's never been folded. By using such paper, it will stay stiff. It must stay stiff to be able to balance it on your fingertip.

Now fold over one corner, as shown in Illus. 194. Make the fold so that it runs diagonally from one corner of the paper to the other. This folding turns the sheet of paper into a triangle.

Don't worry if the paper doesn't form a perfect triangle. Firmly crease the fold you just made. This newly

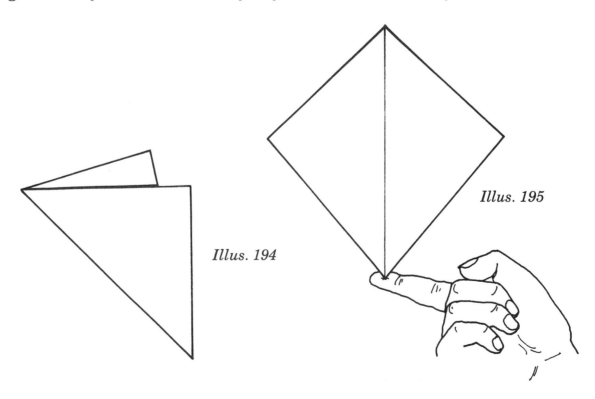

Illus. 194

Illus. 195

creased fold *must* stay in place—the trick depends on this!

Hold the paper with one hand and rest the bottom point of the triangle on the tip of a finger of the other hand. You can place the bottom point in the palm of your hand, instead of on your fingertip. Illus. 195 shows how.

Let go of the paper and keep your fingertip or palm moving with the paper as it tips to one side or to the other. If the fold remains in place (keeping the sheet of paper stiff), you can balance it nicely on your fingertip or in your palm.

Practise keeping your finger or palm directly under the paper's center of gravity and anticipate the direction the paper wants to tip. Don't try this trick where there's a draft, or outdoors in the wind.

Practise this trick on your own until you're certain you know how to keep things balanced. Then challenge others to perform the trick.

Once you feel comfortable using a sheet of notebook paper, experiment with larger sheets of paper.

KEEP YOUR PENCIL ON THE PAPER

Draw a design such as the one shown in Illus. 196 on a small sheet of paper. Show it to your audience.

Tell your audience that you can draw another design very much like the one they're looking at, without lifting your pencil from the paper once you begin drawing.

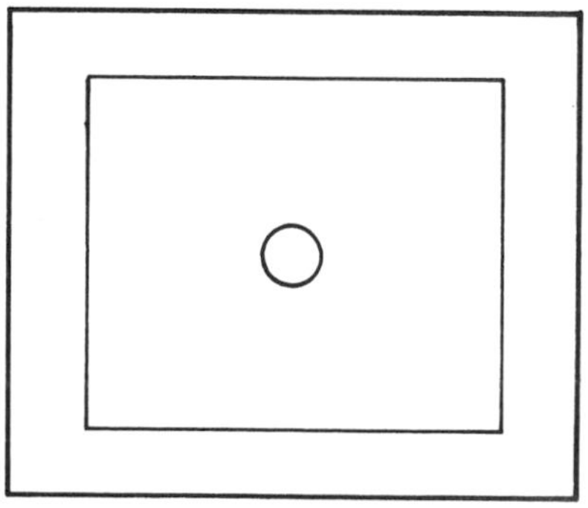

Illus. 196

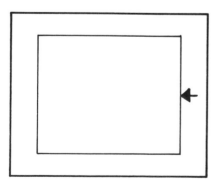

Illus. 197

This is obviously impossible, and your audience will probably tell you so. Once your audience tells you that this trick can't be done, prove to them that it *can*.

Begin by drawing the large outer square. (You could draw a circle, a rectangle, or even a triangle—it's up to you.) Begin and end your drawing at the point shown by the arrow in Illus. 197.

Now for the folding! The two folds you'll be making don't need to be *creased*—they can be more like bends in the paper.

Keep the paper pinned down to the table or to the desk top with the point of your pencil or ballpoint pen. Fold the far edge towards you, along the dotted line shown in Illus. 198.

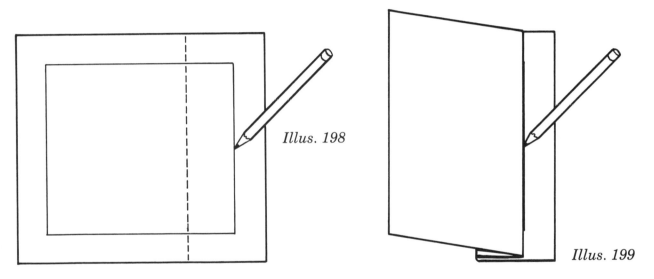

Illus. 198

Illus. 199

Now fold back the end of the paper, away from you, so that the fold comes exactly at the point of your pen or pencil. Illus. 199 shows this fold already in place.

With the paper folded or bent down, carefully push your pen or pencil point up onto the folded section and draw the inside part of your drawing—a circle, a triangle, a square, or anything you choose.

Once this is done, lift your pencil or pen, unfold the paper, and there's the drawing you promised you'd make.

Here's a variation of this same trick. Announce you will draw a figure (a triangle, for example) on the front of your paper, at the right-hand side. Then say that you'll

Can I show you that trick again?

draw *another* figure, a triangle in this case, at the left-hand side of the paper. This triangle, however, will be on the *back* of the paper. You'll accomplish all of this without lifting your pencil from the paper.

Illus. 200 shows the two drawings you'll make. The triangle on the back (the left) is shown drawn with dotted lines because it's not visible from the front.

112

Draw one triangle on the front of the paper. Hold the paper down with the point of your pencil or pen and bend the opposite side of the paper right up to that point. This move is shown in Illus. 201.

Illus. 200

Illus. 201

Draw the second triangle, then lift your pencil or pen. Flatten the paper out, and once again you've performed as promised. You can't play this trick on the same person you tricked with the previous trick. Use one variation of this trick with one audience and the second variation with others.

PAPER SKYHOOK

A skyhook is supposed to be a lifting machine that isn't attached to a support. Skyhooks don't exist, of course. Your *Paper Skyhook* will exist as soon as you make it. What's more, it will give your audience a big surprise.

Tell your audience that you can pick up a partially full two-litre plastic bottle using just a sheet of folded notebook paper. Say that you won't even touch the bottle, only the folded paper will.

To make your *Paper Skyhook*, roll a sheet of notebook paper into a tube 8½″ long, and about ⅜″ across. Roll the paper fairly tight but leave the center hollow. Don't worry if it isn't exactly ⅜″ across. Just don't allow the paper to slip and form a much bigger tube as you roll it.

Fasten the loose edge of the paper using a bit of tape, as shown in Illus. 202. Bend the tube about 2″ from one end, so it looks like the tube shown in Illus. 203.

Now you're ready to pick up a two-litre plastic bottle. Use a smaller bottle if you wish, but be sure it's plastic, with a small mouth. If you drop the bottle you're lifting, it won't break if it's plastic. Begin with an *empty* bottle until you see how your *Paper Skyhook* works.

Tape

Illus. 202   *Illus. 203*

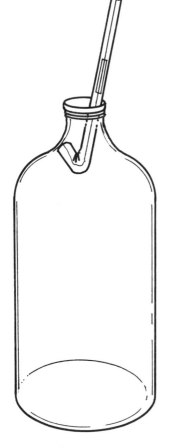

Illus. 204

Push the folded end of the hook into the mouth of the bottle, and then down just a short distance into the bottle's neck. Illus. 204 shows how.

If you push the hook down too far into the bottle, the folded short end will flip open and down into the bottle instead of lodging against the side, as shown in Illus. 204. If the hook opens, pull it out, fold the short end back into place, and then push it back into the bottle again.

Once the short end lodges against the side of the bottle, lift upwards. The bottle will come right up off the table. Remove the hook by pushing it down until the short end unfolds and flips loose. Once the hook is out of the bottle, run a bit of water into the bottle and try to lift it again. If you're careful, you'll find that it's possible to lift a two-litre plastic bottle that's about half full of water. Slowly work your way up to that amount of water. Practise over a sink in case your hook slips!

This is a great trick! What sounds impossible turns out to be really very simple to do, if you know how!

RUBBER PAPER

Cut a sheet of notebook paper in half, so that you have a piece of paper 8½″ by about 5½″. It can be 8″ by 6″, or a bit larger or smaller, so don't worry too much about the exact size.

Fold over the paper along the dotted line shown in Illus. 205. This fold should be about ¼″ wide. If your fold is a bit wider than that, don't be concerned.

The dotted lines shown in Illus. 206 indicate the series of folds you'll make. Just fold over your first fold to make the second. Fold it over again to form the third, and so on, until you've folded your way up the paper.

Illus. 205   *Illus. 206*

Now unfold and flatten out the folded paper and begin to refold it, forming a hollow triangle. Just bend over the first two folds so that the loose edge of paper fits into the third fold. Now you should have a long, slim paper triangle with a bunch of folds extending up from it. Illus. 207 shows this.

Illus. 207

Tape

Illus. 208

Carefully fold the paper over and over along the fold lines so that your triangle gets stronger and stronger as layers of paper build up on it. When you finish, fasten the last loose edge in place, using several strips of tape, as shown in Illus. 208.

A good way to introduce this trick is to hold the tube between your finger and your thumb, very close to one end. Move it up and down a time or two, then remark, "This thing is bending! It must be made of rubber."

Naturally your audience will look to see what you're talking about. The instant you have someone's attention, you will indeed make it look as though the folded-paper triangle is bending or flexing just like rubber.

To make this trick work, hold the paper as shown in the drawing in Illus. 209.

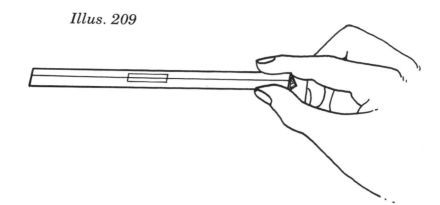

Don't grip the triangle too tightly. Hold it firmly, but loosely enough to allow just a tiny bit of movement.

Shake your hand slightly so that the paper moves up and down, as indicated by the arrows shown in Illus. 210. The dotted lines show the folded paper at the top and bottom of each shake.

Illus. 210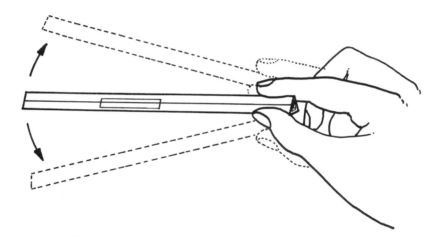

Keep your hand in one position so that the movement is mostly with your fingers and the thumb holding the paper. Just a little up-and-down movement of your fingers and your thumb will create a big swing at the other end of the folded-paper tube.

As you increase the speed that you're moving your hand, you create an optical illusion. Take just a minute to see how this works. What your eyes tell you is that the paper tube is bending. Of course, it isn't. It's just that one end moves in a wide arc and the other end has almost no movement.

Practise this rubber-paper trick until you have a rapid but smooth motion. Check the way the paper looks. Once

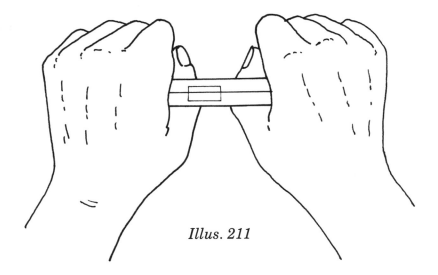

Illus. 211

you know exactly how fast you need to shake your hand,
it's time to perform your latest folded-paper trick!

A great variation of the rubber-paper trick is to hold
the tube between both hands. Illus. 211 shows how this
is done.

Slowly move the outsides of your hands *down*. At the
same time, very slowly lift your thumbs and the part of
your hand nearest your thumbs. The arrows in Illus. 212
show the direction of movement for your hands. It helps
if you seem to strain to "bend" the paper.

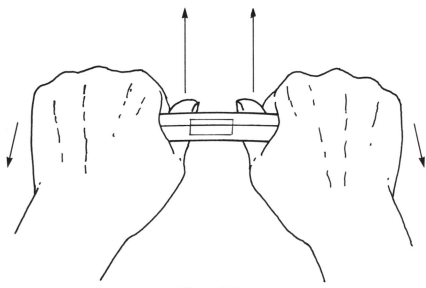

Illus. 212

What makes it seem that the paper tube is bending is an optical illusion. Your speech and expression help make the illusion seem more real.

The folded-paper tube doesn't move or bend at all. What appears to be bending is actually the outside of your hands as they drop and the rest of your hands rise.

Practise this a few times to see how it works. If the folded tube you've been using is too long to fit comfortably (without having it stick out past your hands at either side), just cut it off so it's the proper length. You could fold another tube to the right size, and then keep the longer one for other tricks.

Finish this trick by staring at the tube (it hasn't been bent or creased) and say, "Can you believe that? The paper really does bend just like rubber!"

Older folks will realize how you accomplish this trick. But younger children often see you do it again and again and never figure out how you make the paper tube bend.

SLIPPERY COIN

Did you know that it's easy to push a coin through a hole in a sheet of paper when the hole is smaller than the coin? Begin by drawing a circle the size of a dime on a sheet of paper. Just place a dime (or a penny) in the middle of the sheet of scrap paper and draw a circle around it. Check Illus. 213 to see how this circle looks.

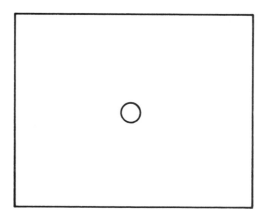

Illus. 213

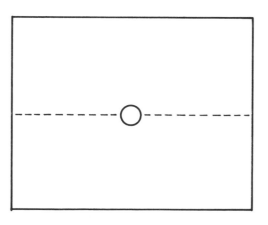

Illus. 214

Very carefully, poke your scissor point through the middle of the circle you drew. Now cut to the line and follow it around the circle. Use tiny little snips so you make a nice, round circle.

Once the circle is cut, it's time to perform your trick. Place a nickel on top of the hole. Look it over and then say, "I can push this nickel through that hole without tearing or cutting the paper."

Your audience will tell you it's impossible. It's time now to show what a tricky person you really are.

Fold the paper so that the fold comes right through the middle of the hole. The dotted line in Illus. 214 shows this fold.

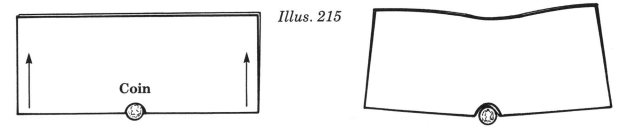

Illus. 215

Illus. 216

Slip the coin inside the folded paper so that the edge of the coin shows through the half circle. Illus. 215 shows how things look at this stage.

Carefully pull or bend both ends of the paper in the direction of the arrows shown in Illus. 215. Gently ease the coin through the hole; the hole expands as the ends of the paper are bent. You may have to coax the coin by nudging it with your finger while you're bending the paper.

The nickel will slide through the hole without tearing the paper. It will look just like Illus. 216 as it passes through the paper.

Afterwards, place the nickel on top of (or beneath) the hole in the paper. Everyone will see that the hole is still smaller than the coin. If you drew your circle around a penny, a quarter will easily pass through the hole in the paper. In fact, if you're very, very carefully, you can coax a quarter through a hole the size of a dime.

Instead of coins, you could use buttons; they'll work just fine. You can even pass jar lids through paper circles that are quite a bit smaller than the lids themselves.

You thought this was impossible, didn't you?

MORE ILLUSIONS

These last two folded-paper tricks are very simple to make. They each will take only a minute or two to fold and cut. The magic of these two tricks lies in the unreliability of the human eye. Although the eye insists that it sees one thing, the human gift of reason knows that it just isn't so!

DO YOU SEE WHAT I SEE?

This folded-paper trick will leave your friends wondering whether or not to believe what they see.

Use a sheet of stiff paper about the size of a sheet of notebook paper or typing paper. The side of a file folder, or a piece of stiff material (a magazine cover or a piece of construction paper) should work perfectly.

Fold the material in half along the dotted line shown in Illus. 217. Once the fold is made, unfold the material.

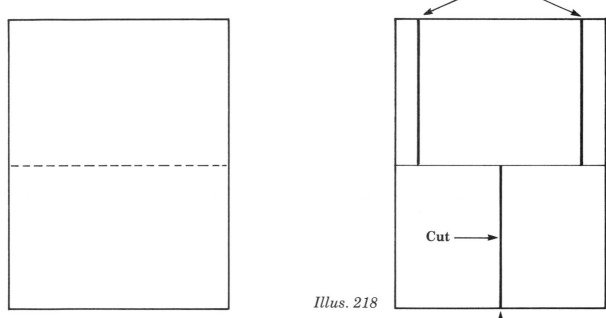

Illus. 218

Illus. 217

Illus. 218 shows three cut lines. Make each of these cuts so they end exactly at the fold you just made. The bottom cut, the one indicated by the arrow, should be halfway between the sides of the material. Don't worry if you're a fraction of an inch closer to one side than to the other. Just try to make the cut in the middle of the material.

The two cuts at the top half of the material should each be about 1″ from the sides of the material.

Illus. 219 shows one section of the paper marked by an "X," and another section is marked by a "Y."

Fold back section "X" under the rest of the page. When you do this, the narrow section above section "X" will

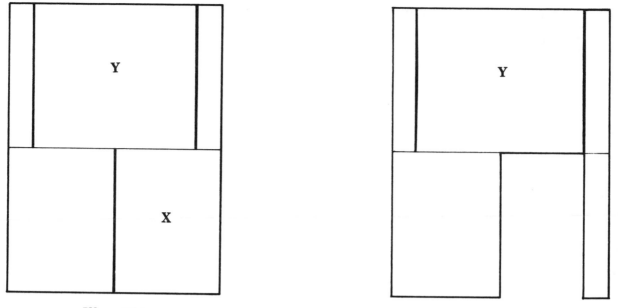

Illus. 219

Illus. 220

come forward. Your folded-paper trick should look just like the one shown in Illus. 220.

Next, fold section "Y" so that it stands straight up. Press the fold so that this wide middle section stands vertically. Now things should look like Illus. 221, when seen from the front.

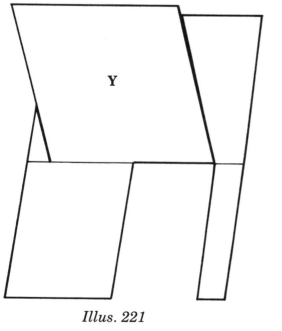

Illus. 221

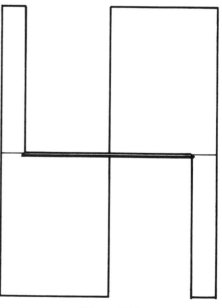

Illus. 222

Illus. 222 is a top view of this great optical illusion. Look at it carefully. Anyone seeing this standing on your desk has to think it's impossible. How can you have cut-out areas on either side of the wide middle section without cutting the middle section itself?

Don't let anyone pick up this illusion and start folding it. Once they do, it's obvious how it works. But just by looking at it, this illusion really seems impossible to believe.

LARGE ONE ON THE RIGHT

All you need for this folded-paper illusion is a sheet of notebook paper, two easy folds, and two quick scissor cuts.

Fold a sheet of notebook paper in half, so that it looks like the one shown in Illus. 223. The dotted line in the drawing shows the next fold. With this second fold in place, your paper should look like Illus. 224.

The first scissor cut is also shown in Illus. 224. Make this cut at the angle shown. Try to judge the cut so that the paper is about two inches wide along the bottom fold, as shown. When this cut is made, your paper should look like Illus. 225.

The second cut, shown in Illus. 225 should be parallel to the first cut. Once you've made this cut, the paper should look like Illus. 226.

Unfold the paper, and you'll have two pieces of exactly the same size. They should both look like the ones shown in Illus. 227.

Here's the funny thing. You know the pieces are exactly the same size. They have to be—you cut them out together! But, when you look at the two side by side, with perhaps 2″ of space between them, the one on the right will appear a bit larger than the one at the left. Try it and see.

Now reverse the two pieces. The one at the right (which was at the left) now seems larger. Of course, this is just an illusion.

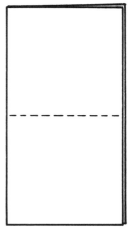

Illus. 223

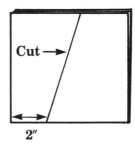

Cut →

2″

Illus. 224

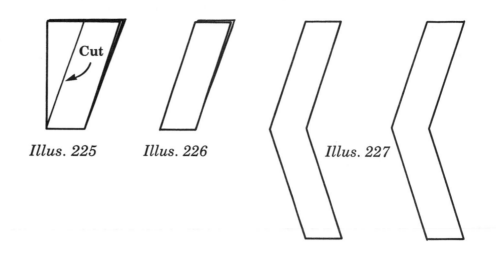

Illus. 225   *Illus. 226*   *Illus. 227*

To put your trick to work, hold the two pieces up side-by-side for your audience to see. Ask which is larger. Your audience will almost always say that the paper to their right is larger. Reverse the pieces and ask which is larger.

This folded-paper trick seems too simple to work, but it does. Almost everyone who sees the pieces side by side will be fooled.

Metric Equivalents

INCHES TO MILLIMETRES AND CENTIMETRES

MM—millimetres   CM—centimetres

Inches	MM	CM	Inches	CM	Inches	CM
⅛	3	0.3	9	22.9	30	76.2
¼	6	0.6	10	25.4	31	78.7
⅜	10	1.0	11	27.9	32	81.3
½	13	1.3	12	30.5	33	83.8
⅝	16	1.6	13	33.0	34	86.4
¾	19	1.9	14	35.6	35	88.9
⅞	22	2.2	15	38.1	36	91.4
1	25	2.5	16	40.6	37	94.0
1¼	32	3.2	17	43.2	38	96.5
1½	38	3.8	18	45.7	39	99.1
1¾	44	4.4	19	48.3	40	101.6
2	51	5.1	20	50.8	41	104.1
2½	64	6.4	21	53.3	42	106.7
2	76	7.6	22	55.9	43	109.2
3½	89	8.9	23	58.4	44	111.8
4	102	10.2	24	61.0	45	114.3
4½	114	11.4	25	63.5	46	116.8
5	127	12.7	26	66.0	47	119.4
6	152	15.2	27	68.6	48	121.9
7	178	17.8	28	71.1	49	124.5
8	203	20.3	29	73.7	50	127.0

INDEX